IT'S ME AGAIN, LORD

VI M. STEARNS

TABLE OF CONTENTS

INTRODUCTION

IT'S ME AGAIN LORD is a conglomeration of true stories that happens in her day to day life, over a period of seven years. The day by day struggles include marriage, divorce, blended families, work ethics, and health, a near death experience, special needs, supernatural meetings, parents, dreams, money, moving, rejection, religion, miracles and much more.

After traveling with her husband in the military for three years, Vi finds herself back in Illinois. At a young age of 22, she is recently divorced. She is left with no home, no money, and an old car to drive. She acquires a part-time job at the local mall, and has to live with her parents, as she tries to pay her bills and feed her young son. Being raised in a Christian home, helps her as she turns to God for answers while facing situations beyond her control.

Many of you will relate to her personal life experiences, as well as be astonished with the outcomes. You will laugh, cry, and gasp with disbelief as you read along. You may be shaken to the core!

I believe it will give hope to the hopeless, and faith to the faithless, as she looks for her rainbow.

PREFACE

Have you ever questioned your Salvation or your Spiritual walk? Does He hear your prayers? Does He really speak to His Children these days?

This is thirty one of my personal stories that have happened in my life.

If I ever questioned His power here on earth, it has been settled. I have reconciled any doubt I ever had that He walks with me and talks with me.

I have come to the conclusion that my life is not my own. He had chosen me, as a young child, to be and do and follow through with His will here on Earth.

I have choices. I can listen to Him & follow through. I can hear but not follow Him. I can do my own thing. Many times I have chosen incorrectly. But even as a young child, I knew I was different.

"I not only marched to a different drummer, I played in my own band" as my Mother would put it. I was always a loner. I was very bright even as a very young child. I always took charge, a teacher, a leader. I learned very quickly anything that was placed before me. Sometimes, I just knew things without being taught. Many questioned things I knew.

The concept of God came easily for me. I prayed for everything, including my cats, dogs, and my family. I even prayed for wild animals, birds, squirrels, rabbits, fish, & even a field mouse once. If there was a question about something, I didn't ask Mom & Daddy, I instinctively asked God.

This wasn't something we talked about in the 1960s. In actuality, few things were ever discussed with children in the 1960s. Children were to be seen and not heard. I was way ahead of the times, according to the adults.

What man called luck, I called miraculous. Read on, and see who you agree with!

RAISE UP A CHILD

I was raised in a home where prayer and miracles were a daily thing. My Daddy, Les, was healed of tuberculosis when I was a young child. My Momma, Doris, was in bed for a year hemorrhaging soon after her last baby was born. She was miraculously healed after the doctor. said there was no cure for what she had.

We were what you might call a poor family in a small town. Momma and Daddy had four children at home (there were six total). Things were tight in the early 60s. Momma rented apartments upstairs, to students for a few years, when we lived in Carbondale. When she heard that a small motel, was in need of a manager, we moved. There was a large house in the back.

Money was still tight. In fact, we wore only hand me down clothes and shoes from cousins. Momma cooked a roast and potatoes on Sunday. We could smell it in the oven when we walked into the house from Church. During the week, we ate fried egg sandwiches when we packed our lunches for school. Sometimes that's all we had. Momma went grocery shopping once a week. She usually had twenty five dollars to spend on groceries and necessities. Sometime we didn't have food in the house. Momma would gather us all in the living room.

"Let's pray! We need food this week!"

I can't count the times within just a few minutes, there'd be a knock on the door. It was a friend, a relative, or even a stranger with a bag of food or money owed to Mom and Dad. I remember a few times, the man who owned the Truck Stop across the street, would give us leftovers from the day's *special*. So we seldom went to bed hungry.

I remember one morning I was rolling Momma's perm, while out on the sidewalk.

"Someday I'm going to Beauty School and make people pretty when I grow up!"

What a dreamer I was! Beauty College was expensive. Few people, besides my Dad, even graduated high school in our family, let alone had money for college tuition. We may not have had a lot of money or things, but we had love in our home. That's what I wanted in my home, too, someday. Someone to love me through thick and thin, 'til death do us part.

I love to cook, sew, and do crafty things. I love Jesus and my family. I love doing for others . . . serving others. I am usually always a joyful person, most of the time happy, and I can be funny too. Most of the time, I'm looking for the, *lighter side of any situation,* just to make a joke. I have always been known as a quick-witted soul. *I could banter back and forth with the guys and gals. Everyone knew that I was just teasing with them. I'm famous for getting in the last word.* But I have a serious side. When it comes to Jesus, The Holy Spirit, and prayer, I'm all serious.

Then there's another side of me. For some reason, many at work called me, "Ann Landers." For those who don't know Ann Landers, she wrote a personal helps column. She was in almost every known newspaper and magazine. There was seldom a day that someone didn't come to me and ask for advice about something. I usually could answer on the spot, but sometimes, I had to do some research first, then get back to them with an answer. It was usually my peers, who would ask advice, not just people younger than me.

I love children. I always told my Mom I was going to grow up and have twenty children. Well, when I realized I was not a *well* person, when I was pregnant, *that* idea went straight out of the window. That just wasn't going to happen the way I thought.

I had my own ideas about everything. I always thought *outside the box* and seemed to be way ahead of the pack, doing everything in business before it was popular. Making friends came easy, but truly trusting people was difficult for me, at this point in my life.

Follow me through the years, as God opens one door as He undoubtedly closes another.

I have always believed in living from day to day. I have seldom planned anything new in the week. I kept busy with family and work. I wasn't ever one to ask anyone to do anything for me, I'd just figure it out, and do it myself. I was an independent soul from the word GO! I wasn't really interested in movies or running around with a crowd.

In fact, I didn't really have a crowd to run with. I not only march to the beat of my own drum . . . I play in my own band!

I had been living out of state for the past three years, while my husband was in the Army. We came back to Illinois when his tour of duty was finished. We were home for about eight months when we separated, and soon divorced. I had no choice, but to move in with my parents for a few months, while I got back on my feet. I had a young son to look out for. He loved staying at Grandma and Grandpa's house. There really wasn't room for us, but Mom put a rollaway bed in the dining room for me, Stevie Bear slept on the couch. I had called him Little Bear since I found out I was pregnant. As he learned to talk, when we'd asked him, "What's your name little boy?"

He would merely answer, "Me Bear!"

When we moved back to Illinois, he said, "Grandpa and Grandma calls me Stevie Bear . . . so I want you to call me Stevie Bear too."

So from that day on, he was Stevie Bear or just Bear.

The divorce went through in August (on my ex's birthday). *Happy Birthday!* He received the divorce papers two days later, on the date which would have been our anniversary. *Happy Anniversary!* I was glad it was over, but I was scared of the future at the same time. What would happen to me, to us? Was there ever going to be a light at the end of the tunnel? *Where's my rainbow?* Would I ever find true love?

I had been a *battered wife* and I had recently found out Stevie Bear had been abused also. As a Christian, I had always prayed for my ex-husband and thought that he would one day change. He obviously didn't. I didn't really believe in divorce, but after what I'd lived through in my marriage, it was necessary to do so. Actually, it was a miracle I was still alive!

Be still before the Lord and wait patiently for Him. (Psalm 37:7)

Jesus said, "Blessed are the peacemakers, for they will be called sons of God. (Matthew 5:9)

ACCUSED

One morning, I woke up crying. I was feeling lonely, and I started praying and asking, "God, what do I do now? Where do I go from here?" I tried to be quiet, as it was early in the morning.

About that time, I heard little pitter patter on the bare floor. It was my son, Stevie Bear. "What's wrong, Mommy?"

I opened my eyes. He must have heard me crying softly. He handed me a tissue. The soft light from the bathroom shined throughout part of the room. Bear put his little hand up to my face.

"Mommy's sad today," I whispered as he leaned over and laid his head on my pillow.

"Don't be sad, Mommy. I know you miss Daddy too, but I'm here! I'll take care of you from now on, Mommy! Don't worry!"

I bit my tongue trying not to just burst out in tears. He was so sweet and being so grown-up at that moment. I just hugged him and snuggled with my Little Bear until we both went back to sleep.

I was awakened by my Daddy making a pot of coffee in the percolator. I put on my housecoat and joined him at the table. About that time, Momma came into the kitchen.

"Who wants breakfast?" she asked cheerfully.

"I'll just have toast and coffee. I'm not feeling well today."

Dad turned to Momma, "We are talking, Honey. Wait just a little while, then I'll have some breakfast."

I finished my toast and coffee, and went in to get ready for work.

I had been working at Walgreens Drug Store in the mall, soon after we had gotten out of the Army and moved back to Illinois. Things weren't working out well there, but I went in anyways with my usual cheerful attitude. I wasn't working full time yet, so there were no benefits. I even went to Public Assistance at one point. I jumped through *all of their hoops,* and was still turned down.

A few weeks passed and I got a phone call one morning from them. "If you will pay us $650.00 per month, we can give you a medical card, just for your son."

I felt my face flush as I talked to the woman on the phone. *"I don't even make $650.00 a month!"*

She said, "If you'll quit working and stay home with your son, we could help more. But, you are working, sorry."

I thanked her and hung up the phone. I liked working, I just wanted something to help in case Stevie Bear got sick or hurt.

I got along with everyone at work, so I thought. Then one day a coworker told me at lunchtime, "Someone has been stealing cash. I heard them talking in the office today."

After lunch, one of the assistant managers took me to the stockroom. He said, "I'm sorry to have to tell you this, but . . .

Because you are recently divorced and you are driving an older car, *you* must have taken the cash out of the drawer, because you need money. The manager thinks *you* are the one stealing."

I was shocked! "You're kidding right? How much is missing?" I asked.

"$40.00." he answered, looking down shuffling his feet.

You want to see this little German girl get mad? Accuse me of stealing or lying to you! I stormed out of the stockroom.

I went straight to the office where the store manager was sitting at his desk. *"You accused me of stealing? Well, let me set the record straight! I have never stolen anything from anyone and I'm not going to start now! I have never and won't ever steal from you! . . . and I won't ever steal for you! Also, I won't ever lie to you! And I won't ever lie for you! But obviously you don't trust me! I can't work for someone who doesn't trust me! Well, you won't have to worry about me anymore! I quit!"* I turned around to walk down the steps, I looked back and said, *"Oh and by the way . . . if I was going to take something and go to jail for it . . . it sure as heck wouldn't be a measly $40.00!"* I took off my work smock and threw at him.

I went next door, cleared out my locker, and threw my things in the back of my car. I could barely see going home. I was scared, angry, hurt, and confused. I prayed out loud, "Lord, You have to help me now! I can't deal with a liar and a thief! I am being accused of stealing! You know I just got away from my husband who thought those were both were fine, but *not me!*" I drove home still crying.

It was late when I got home, Momma and Daddy were gone to bed already. I kissed Stevie as he slept on the couch.

I later heard they caught the girl who was stealing. I eventually got an apology from one of the assistant managers.

THE TICKET

The next day I woke up, after a fitful night's sleep. Momma was gone to town. Daddy was busy working in the garage. *Me, I didn't have a job!*

"I don't have a job!" I said out loud. I've never been fired from any job I've had. I was still upset for being accused of such petty stuff . . . and I almost got fired for something I didn't do! I really thought they knew me better than that!

There was a little restaurant down the street. I grabbed a paper and a cup of coffee. There was nothing in there that I was interested in.

I finished my coffee and drove to see a friend, Jenny. I hadn't seen her since I'd been back in Illinois. I used to work with her at a restaurant in another town. She hugged me, as I walked in her house. *"What are you doing in town? I have been trying to find your number!"*

She immediately showed me her ring on her finger. *"I'm engaged!"* she squealed. We went in and sat down on the couch. She told me all about how she met James, and they *hit it off right away! I was so excited for her!* She was kind of a "hippie" in school. It was the 70's though. *She always said she would never, ever, ever get married! No tie downs for her!* Not Jenny!

"Oh and I'm working at the local golf course as a waitress. We're looking for another good waitress. I thought of you! That's funny that you came by today, I didn't have your number anymore!"

She called her boss and set up an interview for that day. That afternoon I went in for the interview, got my aprons, and went to work the next day at 6am. They laughed at me because *I said I didn't drink liquor of any kind! In fact, I couldn't stand the smell of whiskey or beer!* I was told I would have to serve it though.

I had worked in one place where I served bottled beer. I personally don't like it, but I can serve it. They all got a kick out of it when they saw me *cringe and shiver when it splashed on me, as I filled a chilled mug from the tap!*

Many times the customers would say, *"I'll buy you a drink!"* I was told, rather than saying *Sorry, I don't drink*, just pour something in a glass, even if it's a Coke. My favorite was 7-Up with a cherry & an orange slice on a sword. Or sometimes I'd change it up and put an olive on the sword. I'd walk around and sip on it all night. Only my coworkers really knew my secret. I worked there all summer.

One hot summer night, our ice maker went down. The sheriff asked me for the keys to my car to run into town and get bags of ice. I had a small station wagon.

I tossed him the keys, *"If you wreck it, make sure it's totaled!"*

He just laughed. He left, and came back 30 minutes later with the whole back-end of my car filled with bags of ice. He kind of grinned at me as he handed me the keys. "You're driving a real bomb!" he said.

I agreed, *"Yes, it is, but it gets me around!"*

My little Pinto wagon had a lot of miles on it. Dad said it was a four cylinder running on only two cylinders. Therefore, it wouldn't go over 40 mph. even on a bet! I didn't care, I didn't drive fast to begin with.

We both laughed as I helped him unload the bags of ice. We got it all carried in and put away. I continued waiting on all the customers, helped with clean-up and closed.

On morning I was on my way to work, I had to pass through a small town. I drove to the stop sign, turned left, and drove a couple of blocks. A lady in a big, long, gold Lincoln Continental, made a complete stop, and then made a right hand turn into the gas station parking lot. I had to come to a complete stop too. I wasn't in a big hurry, but it was early and I had to be to work in thirty minutes.

As I put my foot on the gas, and was going out of town, an old blue Chevy pick-up passed me. I was barely out of town. I looked down, noticed I was up to 35 mph. About that time, a police officer came roaring up behind me, light flashing, and sirens blaring. I figured he was after the truck who had just passed me. We had both pulled over. The policeman pulled up between our vehicles. Just then the truck just pulled out onto the road, and took off . . . leaving me with the police officer.

He came up to the window, *"Are you in a big hurry, Little Missy?"*

"No not really. I'm just on my way to work. I figured you saw that truck pass me back there."

"*No! You are the one I'm after!*" He smiled as he took my driver's license back to his squad car.

I have never been pulled over, because I am a very safe driver. He was gone for about ten minutes. When he came back, he handed my license back, "*I'm going to teach you a lesson!*"

"*So . . . what did I do, Sir? I couldn't possibly have been speeding!*"

"*Oh yes, Little Lady, I clocked you at fifty five, in a thirty!*" He wrote out the ticket and handed it to me.

"*But,*" I started to say.

He interrupted me, "*I clocked you on my radar gun! No buts!*" He turned around and walked back to his squad car.

I started my car and carefully pulled out on the road. "*Lord, what are you trying to tell me? I really need some help with this one! I can't possibly afford a ticket! And you know I didn't do anything!*"

I put the ticket in my pocket and continued on to work. Later that day, the sheriff came in. "I'm going to have the usual," he sat down at the bar.

"*Coming right up!*" I said, as I got his drink and put his order in at the kitchen.

"*Guess what I got this morning?*" I stopped near his barstool.

"*I don't know. What did you get?*"

"I got a speeding ticket! The first one I've ever had in my life!" I pulled it out of my pocket.

He started laughing. "Wait! Let me guess. I'll bet it was from the guy in that little town you pass through coming to work." Then he named the officer.

"How did you know?" I handed the ticket to him.

"Because he notoriously looks for women by themselves, driving early in the morning and late at night! I hear about him all the time!"

Then he started laughing even harder. *"Hey, Vi! Were you in that little Pinto wagon, when he pulled you over?"*

Of course I said I was.

"You bring that ticket into my office in the morning. I'll take care of it for you! I drove that little bomb of yours to get ice the other night. It wouldn't get over forty mph even when I floored it! You couldn't have possibly been going fifty five!" And with that statement, he had everyone around him laughing.

I went into the kitchen, got his order and took it to him. I whispered, *"Thank you, Lord for having the sheriff drive my car the other night!"*

I drove to the sheriff's office the next day. He gave my license back, and dismissed the ticket. I thanked him and drove on to work.

LADIES DAY

Summer was almost over. I was really thinking I'd just continue working through the winter since I had learned my job well. I even filled in a few times behind the bar. I really had no idea about mixed drinks, but there were two little books behind the bar, the manager showed me one day. If I ever needed to be the bartender, I could use the recipes in the books to mix drinks, cocktails, etc.

Today was Ladies Day . . . golf, drinks and lunch for about forty women. Jenny and I were setting up tables for the day. Filling salt and pepper shakers, ketchup and mustards, wrapping silverware, etc. It had to be done before each shift.

About that time, the phone rang. I got up to answer it.

"Susan was supposed to bartend today, but she called in sick, so I have to work the bar today!" I said to Jenny as we folded the silverware in napkins. Jenny was waitressing with me that day.

She leaned over and whispered to me, *"The room will be full of ladies. Oh my gosh! I don't know how I'm going to serve them all by myself! I don't usually work on Ladies Day!"*

"Don't worry. I can help you. I'll take half of the room, if you like. They always start with a round of drinks as they play cards anyways."

"I'll help you make drinks, if you help me wait on them."

"*Great!*" as I rolled my eyes.

I was soon to experience my first time behind a bar. We took the ladies' drink orders. While Jenny helped me with the drink orders, we divided up the room for serving the ladies their lunches.

"*To save time on refills, I suggest we serve all drinks in brandy snifters! The food orders would be easy today anyways, we have a special on the menu!*" I said to Jenny.

We served the ladies' their drinks and took their orders. We had to wait awhile before serving their lunches, in order for them to finish a round of cards.

We soon got the thumbs up sign from Mrs. Spiller, the leader of the group, to start serving lunches.

Most of the ladies had finished their drinks, so I went back behind the bar and made *another round*.

As we served the food to each of the ladies, *I heard so many women say that these were the best drinks they'd ever had here!* We just smiled and continued serving lunches.

Lunch was soon over, Mrs. Spiller motioned us to clear tables.

Another round of drinks for the room, as they played one more round of cards.

We took the tubs of dishes into the kitchen, poured ourselves a Coke from the tap, and took a break. After this group leaves, we can eat our lunches and get ready for the next group to come in.

The ladies seemed to be getting *unusually* louder by the minute. *All of a sudden we heard a blood curdling scream coming from the room. Jenny and I dropped what we were doing and ran to see what was going on!*

We were not prepared for what we saw in that room! The lady that screamed was crawling around on her hands and knees on the floor, under the big round oak table. *I ran over towards her.*

She screamed, *"I dropped my glasses! I can't find my glasses!"* She was frantic!

I was cautioned by one of the ladies at the table to not come nearer. She was about to fall off of her chair. All of the ladies were pretty well plastered to put it mildly.

One lady, who was quietly shuffling a deck of cards, stood up and flipped the whole deck into the air! She announced, *"I'm done! I've lost all of my money!"*

One lady at the back of the room was leaned up against the wall sound asleep, with her drink still clutched tightly in her hand. All of a sudden, (a lady at the first table) screamed, *"You touched my leg! Get off of my leg!"* at the lady still crawling around under the table. A red-haired lady started belly-laughing. Now you would have to know her, a real *Miss Straight Lace,* if you know what I mean.

She looked at me as she exclaimed, *"Turn the music up! I want to dance!"*

With that remark, the whole room let loose in loud, roaring laughter.

I heard from someone, *"We have never had this much fun here before! I love this place!"*

A couple just laughed and rolled on the floor.

Another lady finally went under the table to try and help the other to get back up to her chair.

She started laughing, *"I'm stuck!"* She had somehow gotten her foot stuck under the table leg, and it pulled her shoe off.

I couldn't stand there anymore . . . I was trying to hold my composure, and not laugh at them. I just turned around and left the room.

The cook came out of the kitchen to see if we were ok. Jenny and I assured her that we were.

Jenny said, "I have their husbands' phone numbers. Their time is up, anyway."

We called their husbands to come and get their girls.

"Your wife isn't in any shape to drive. Please come and get her." I said to each one. I called as many as I could.

When the guys came to pick up their wives, some were embarrassed, while some of the others just said, *"Parr for the course!"*

"Oh well, It's Ladies Day, but I've never seen her like this!" said Henry.

"What was she drinking?" asked Gregg, as he carried his wife out.

One by one they left the room.

We cleaned up the messy room and got ready for the next group to come in.

We were short handed, so Jenny and I pulled double shift that day. Some of the men were still laughing when they came in that evening for golf and drinks.

I was looking to be reprimanded by some of them for serving the girls so much to drink. How was I supposed to know there were different types of glasses for different drinks? I didn't drink! I just thought we could *save some time* on refills. I decided then that I never wanted to be a bartender. Jenny and I had a big laugh, as we counted out our tips for the day. We finished the second shift and went home.

Oh, and by the way, about the lady, who was crawling on the floor . . . *Of course her glasses had been on top of her head, the whole time!*

I heard later, from some of the men, that few of the women *didn't even remember being there,* that day! I think others are still trying to forget the day, *I drank them under the table!*

CAMP FIRE

The months passed quickly. Stevie Bear started Kindergarten. Staying with Mom and Dad made it easy for me while I worked. It was so helpful that Momma or Daddy could take him to school and back at noon.

One evening I got home. Bear was sitting in the corner.

"*What's wrong?*" I put down my purse and pulled off my jacket.

"*Well, evidently, it is Smokey the Bear week at school. He brought all of his papers home today. But he also went by Grandpa's shop and wiped away all of the rocks, then placed some bigger rocks in a circle. Then he laid a bunch sticks in a cross pattern in the middle. Then he got some of Grandpa's matches and lit it on fire! If Grandpa hadn't come around the building, he might have gotten hurt! He was covering it up with some dirt and rocks! So I made him sit in the corner.*"

I looked at Stevie, he looked away and whimpered.

"*Steven, why would you do such a thing? Fire is dangerous! You know that! It will burn you!*"

Then Mom interjected, "*The bad part was . . . he built the fire under the backend of a customer's car!*"

"Oh my God! How in the world? Why? Mom, you just described a campfire! How would he know how to build a campfire?" I looked at Mom.

"I don't know, but I'd go talk with the teacher about this, if I were you! Maybe she knows something about it!"

So the next morning, I took Stevie Bear to school. I checked in to the Principal Don's Office. I told him the story. He called the teacher into the office.

"Miss Smith, please explain to me how a five year old knows how to make a campfire?" Then he repeated to her, what I'd told him about the fire.

"Well, after I read the story about Smokey the Bear, I took the kids outside and built a campfire in the gravel. Then we all threw dirt and rocks on it to put it out, and I took the kids back inside," said Miss Smith. *I just stood there in disbelief . . . Did I just hear her say she showed the kids how to build a campfire and then put it out? I was mad!*

I looked at her and said sternly, *"No five year old needs to know how to start a fire . . . let alone how to put one out! All they need to know is if they ever see a fire, to run and get an adult! What were you thinking?"*

About that time the phone rang. It was Mrs. Taylor who lived down the street from Mom and Dad.

The secretary told the Principal, "Mrs. Taylor is on the phone. She says her daughter burned their camping trailer down last night. When she questioned Angela, she said, *"Miss Smith showed us how!"*

Principal Don now knew this was not an isolated case now. Tell her I'll call her right back." he said. *"I'll make sure Miss Smith never, ever does that again! Isn't that right, Miss Smith?"*

Miss Smith looked a little shaken, *"I thought that the kids would just learn how to build a fire, not just to put one out!"* she replied to him.

"Five year olds! They are just babies! You obviously don't have children!" I raised my voice a little. *"I need to go now. Thank you for your time. I hope this never happens again!"*

I left the office and went back to Mom's. Dad was going into the house as I was driving into the driveway. He poured me a cup of coffee as we mulled over the whole story. I told him and Mom about little Angie Taylor burning down her parents' travel trailer. They couldn't believe it!

I looked up, *"Thank you God, for watching out for our little Bear and for sparing the customer's car!"*

Mom and Dad both said, *"Amen!"*

A LITTLE HYPER

Stevie had just had his fifth birthday, in July, a month before school started. Grandma had bought him a *bow saw* for his birthday. *I was not impressed!* But Mom said she bought it so he could help Grandpa when a branch fell out of one of the trees.

Stevie Bear was stronger than most children his age. He lifted things and carried buckets of water to water the rose bushes with ease. So, cutting up little branches seemed normal to Mom. She was teaching him to help Grandpa and keeping Stevie busy too.

He was one of those kids who just couldn't sit still. I would get a note from Miss Smith . . . *Please tell* Stevie *he can't talk in class . . . or . . . Please tell Stevie he has to stay in his seat while at school.* I thought that was her job!

Then one day I got a note . . . *Please make an appointment for Stevie to see a Psychologist. He says he's missing his Daddy and acting out at school.*

I called a child Psychologist, he saw him, and immediately put him on Ritalin.

Within two days . . . *Oh my God! I never saw Stevie so hyperactive! He couldn't sleep at night, he talked ninety miles a minute, and he couldn't even sit and eat at the table any more.*

I called the Psychologist and told him what was going on. "He will get used to it. It will take about a week," he told me.

After a month on Ritalin, he continued to not sleep at night, which made him tired at school. I finally, just didn't take him back to that doctor.

Next idea? Anyone? I was worn completely out! I worried about him every day and night. What was he going to do next? My ex-husband had abused him and me. I was finally away from him. I realized we would both have to go through some mental, and emotional healing, and some other things, we just didn't understand.

I was slowly healing, both physically and mentally, mostly through prayer and talking with my Mom and Dad.

In fact, I was at church one Sunday Morning. I had told a lady about my circumstances. She suggested that *I was being punished by God for getting a divorce.*

I found myself at the altar crying and praying for forgiveness for getting divorced.

"As clearly as if God was standing next to me, I heard, *"Daughter, you don't need forgiveness for getting a divorce, I forgive you for being married!"*

"What?" I thought. I was puzzled. I opened my eyes and looked around me. There was no one near me there. I was dumbfounded! I had never heard anyone preach on being forgiven for being married . . .

I got up from the altar with a new perspective. I never asked Him to forgive me for being divorced again! I would never carry condemnation for that again!

I knew God had spoken it to me that morning.

POPSICLE STICKS

I didn't really have a friend to talk to, about my personal trials. After being out of state most of my married life, I hadn't made very many friends since high school. I did have a co-worker, Karla, that I'd grown close to. We had similar divorce stories. I had gone to school with her twin brothers. We would talk about our past and we shared a lot of personal things. She had remarried and just had a new baby girl. It was healing to me to see she was happy now. It gave me hope for my future. She would always give Stevie Bear a Popsicle, when we visited.

One day we were visiting her and the baby at their house. Karla handed Bear a Popsicle and told him to sit on the porch and eat it. We checked on him every few minutes to see how he was doing with that Popsicle. We were drinking coffee and chatting and admiring her tiny baby in the cradle in the living room.

I got up to check on Bear, *"Karla, come look at this!"* We peered out the screen door in amazement!

Bear had finished his Popsicle and he had taken the two sticks and *edged* both sides of the sidewalk!

"He did a better job than the guy I pay to do the lawn!"

Stevie came up to the door.

"Look! I fixed it for you!" he proudly held up his Popsicle sticks.

I had him come in and wash his hands. She gave Bear five dollars for his piggy bank and for doing such a good job on her sidewalk.

He had his times when he was loud, but he also had a tender side. He loved animals and babies. Anyone who was younger than himself, he considered a baby! He was like an adult stuck in a child's body!

THE FENCE AND THE FIREFIGHTERS

I came home from work one evening. Mom and Dad were watching TV in the living room. Stevie Bear was squished in between them, holding a huge bowl of popcorn. Mom got up and met me in the dining room.

"Stevie's in trouble again, today!"

"Now what did he do?"

"Well, we got a call from Mr. Conner next door. He had us meet him at the fence. Stevie had taken the bow saw and very carefully cut about eighteen inches out of each of the fence rails! *He has threatened to sue us, if we don't replace the whole fence!"*

"I don't think he can legally make us replace the whole fence. A fence is put up in lengths of wood. We will just have to replace the wood, or fix what he cut out. I'll talk to Mr. Conner tomorrow."

I prayed to God that night that Mr. Conner would be in a better mood tomorrow. And that he wouldn't threaten a lawsuit with us. I didn't make enough money to fix a fence.

First thing in the morning, I saw Mr. Conner standing at the fence shaking his head. I walked over to him.

"Look at what that boy of yours did to my fence!" he said curtly.

"Yeah, Mom told me about it last night," I said, as I looked at the four missing fence pieces.

"How old is your fence, Mr. Conner? I'll have to wait for another week until I get paid, but I'll replace it with new boards."

He looked down at the missing pieces. Next to the fence, Stevie had stacked the wood neatly in a pile.

"I noticed they were all exactly the same length!" All of a sudden his facial expression changed, *"I have never seen anybody cut so perfectly straight lines like that! Have you?"* he laughed. *"Aww, heck! Stevie Bear is my little buddy! I can't be mad at him for this. The fence was old anyways! In fact, I think I can fix it without buying any new wood. Don't worry about it!"*

I thanked him and invited him over for coffee sometime, as I walked back across the lawn.

"That's not how he was yesterday! He was mad!"

That afternoon, Daddy got some nails and helped Mr. Conner fix the fence.

The cuts were so straight, they just went back into place and they stabilized them. It didn't take them long. Stevie Bear and Mr. Conner became closer friends after that little incident. *Of course, he had to promise to never do that again!*

A few weeks passed. One morning we heard the storm siren go off in town. Soon the sky turned dark, the winds blew eighty mph, as the rain poured down in sheets. We all went into the house and got under the table until it passed. The electricity popped loudly, and the lights went out. When the storm passed by, we all went out to see what had happened. Dad noticed a tree behind the garage had been uprooted and was leaning against another tree, keeping it from falling on the garage roof. Other than debris in the yard, from the neighbor, and the trash barrels turned over, we had no damage.

Praise the Lord! God had spared our little home from the nasty storm!

The police and the firefighters came by to check on us. They were going door to door and assessing the damage. They were also checking for gas leaks and trees that had fallen on houses.

We found out later it was a tornado type storm that came thru our little town. It knocked out all of the electricity for many days, and almost every house in town had huge trees down in the yards.

It was such a mess, but Stevie Bear went right to work. He got his little bow saw out and started cutting up the limbs and branches into the same perfect lengths, that he had cut Mr. Conner's fence, just a few weeks before. He stacked fifteen limbs neatly in intricate piles on the boulevard.

Grandma made a little sign, *FIREWOOD $5.00*. He placed it in front of the piles.

A couple of the city police and firefighters drove by, one day, and saw Bear working in the yard. They stopped and asked him what he was doing?

He replied, *"The storm came and messed up the whole town! I'm helping the town clean up!"* He continued cutting and stacking his little wood piles so meticulously.

We lived right on the highway. Every day there were hundreds of cars passing by. The piles of wood were being sold almost as fast as he could cut and stack them.

The firefighter came down one day, while he was cutting wood. He asked if it was okay to take him downtown and show him the firetruck. They said they had been watching him hard at work, and felt that he needed to be honored somehow. We went down to the fire station. They gave us the grand tour of the fire house. They strapped a helmet on Stevie Bear's head and one of them pinned a badge on him. They put us on the firetruck and gave us the tour of the town, lights on, sirens blaring intermittently, as we made our way up and down the streets, like we were in a *Grand Parade*.

We were taken back to the station, where Stevie Bear was given an orange soda and some homemade cookies. The firefighters and the police in town came over and shook Bear's little hand. Each one thanked him for doing his part in cleaning up the town. The Chief presented Stevie with a "Jr. firefighter badge, fire hat, and a certificate". We celebrated for a little while, then we were taken back home. Stevie Bear was so proud to be one of the *"fire guys"* as he referred to them.

I went to work that night with stories to tell everyone. I had no idea they had been watching my little five year old working in the yard. In the weeks following, the *"fire guys"* would bring Bear a limb or two, from what they were picking up, in the area yards. That way, he wouldn't run out of work. It kept him very busy for quite a while.

One lady, from a neighboring town, stopped by and ordered a whole truck load of wood, if he could cut it a little bigger for her fireplace. He had fun cutting the wood. She came by a week later and filled her truck with the limbs cut perfectly for her fireplace. He was paid quite well for the truckload. He even got to help load it up on the truck! Bear loved being outside. He was out of school for Christmas break. I started looking for a place to move to, before the end of the year, but my car broke down. I had to use my funds to fix my transmission instead. Oh well, another time.

I HAVE A JOB, THANK YOU

I got a call at work from Momma. She said softly, "Honey, Ma Ripley has passed away. The funeral will be in a few days. You may have to get off work for the funeral."

"I'll trade days with Jenny. She won't mind, Mom."

Ma was really my great-aunt, not my grandmother. She and Pa had raised my Mom as a young child. They were the only grandparents I knew, as a child. We were really close to her and Pa.

At the young age of seven, I would stand on a stool and wrap her hair in perm rods. Yes, I was an aspiring young hairdresser, even as a child. After I'd perm her hair, she had me trim it up with the special silver handled scissors she kept in her roller box. Then, I'd roll her hair on brush rollers, as she sat under her tabletop hair dryer. I'd brush her hair into beautiful waves and spray it with Aqua Net Hairspray. Ugh! *I can still smell that stinky, sticky hairspray, but Ma loved it! What Ma wanted, Ma got!*

When her hair was finished, I was always treated to a big, ice cold glass of her special sweet tea from the glass jars in the back of the fridge. She would also give me a big hug and kiss on the cheek.

She would slip two or three dollars into my hand and say, "Buy yourself something nice!" That would buy me a new blouse or even a pair of shoes in the 1960's.

Deb, a good friend of mine, called *"Vi, I have an interview tomorrow! There's a new store coming to town! My car is in the shop for another week! Could you possibly take me to the Unemployment Office?"*

"I'll be in town for Ma's funeral. I'll come by and pick you up afterward though. *See you tomorrow!"* We agreed on that and hung up the phone.

Mom, Dad, and I attended Ma's funeral. There were so many people there. I hadn't seen some of my cousins and their children in years, and some of the babies I had never met.

After the funeral, I told Mom I was going to pick up Deb, and that I would be by to visit with the family in just an hour or two.

I left the house and drove to Deb's house. She was ready to go when I arrived. She was dressed in black. I was also dressed in black, from head to toe, due to just coming from the funeral.

We walked in. The place was packed. We found two chairs near the far end of the room and sat down. We chatted a few minutes about the kids. She had a little girl and I had a little boy close to the same age. They enjoyed playing together when we visited. I had been out of state for a few years, but we got together when I'd come home. We planned to get together the next day for a play date with the kids.

A young man walked out and announced, "Those of you here for the Walmart jobs, please come this way." Everyone got up and left the room, leaving me by myself.

I pulled a book out of my purse to read while I waited.

About fifteen minutes passed, I was starting to get hungry, and I'd only drank one cup of coffee before the funeral. About that time, a door opened and a short, gray-haired man, in a really nice light gray suit, came out of one of the rooms. The door slammed behind him, echoing in the empty room. I glanced at him out of the corner of my eye. I continued reading. He walked past me, his heels clicking on the floor as he walked. He paused at the magazines on the table just past me. He turned around and walked slowly walked past me again.

He hesitated, turned and smiled at me, *"Hello, it's a mighty fine day we have today!"*

"I looked up from my book, "Yes, it is," I replied, smiling up at him.

Our words seemed to resonate throughout the room. He walked back to the room that he came from, his shoes clicking all the way. He opened the door, and entered the room as the door once more slammed loudly behind him. I continued reading my book.

About twenty minutes passed, and I heard the door open once more. Click, click, click, click, he walked toward my chair. This time he deliberately stopped. "Hi, are you here for a job?" he asked quietly.

"No, I have a job. I just brought a friend for her interview. My grandma passed away. I just came from her funeral." My eyes filled suddenly with tears as I spoke.

He handed me the white handkerchief from the lapel pocket of his suit. I wiped my eyes. I tried to hand it back, he said "*Keep it. I have hundreds!*" He grinned, trying to get a smile out of me. "*Come back here with me. I want to talk with you. You want a cup of coffee?*" he said, as I followed him into the room. He handed me a cup of coffee, as I sat at the table in the middle of the room. He poured himself a cup also, and sat across from me.

He stated, "We are opening a new variety store here in a couple of weeks. Have you ever heard of Walmart? We have everything from candy to tires. We are hiring people to work in all departments. Right now we are starting the "setup" just north of town."

I again explained, "*Wal-what? No, I've never heard of that!* I just brought my friend here. In fact, I have a good job. I like it where I am. I have a little boy and I have been just recently divorced." I felt tears well up in my eyes once more. I fought them back.

He looked at me, "*I really want you to work for us! I'll tell you what! You can be over any department you want. I just feel that you are supposed to work for us. You are just the type of person we are looking for! I'll bet you have great people skills!*" He continued, "*We will offer you insurance as a full time associate. We will eventually have a retirement plan put into place and our associates will be able to purchase shares in the company. If you'd like a job, show up on Monday morning at 8:00, at the opposite end of the Kroger building just north of town!"*

I was familiar with the place. But I had not been out that way for quite a while. I didn't know they were building a new store. It sounded nice, but I really wasn't wanting to change jobs yet. I liked waitressing.

"I'll think about it," I smiled at him, finished my coffee and got up to leave. He rushed to open the door for me, just in time.

The far door opened, and the group exited from another room. I walked outside. Deb found me and we went to the car. As I drove her back to her house, I told her what the man had told me. She was so excited, she hadn't worked for a long time.

"So, are you going to go Monday? I won't know if I got the job or not, until tomorrow. *They'll call* me . . . but *I think I got it!"* She got out of the car.

"I really doubt it. I like it at the Country Club. I really don't want to change jobs right now!"

"I'll see you and Stevie in the morning! Come by for breakfast if you want to! I'll be up around nine!"

I waved and drove to the venue where Mom and Dad were visiting the family. They had Stevie Bear with them. I told Mom all about the gray-haired man in the suit.

"Insurance would be nice for you and Bear. You know there isn't *any* where you work now."

"I know! I'm just now feeling like I know everyone, and I mostly know where everything is! I'd just be starting over

learning a new job again! I dislike starting over! I do catch on quickly, and it's easy for me to memorize things and learn new names! Anyways, I have all weekend to think about it!"

We visited with the family for a while, then left for home. I popped in a tape of Elvis and sang along. It was breezy that afternoon, the leaves were just starting to change colors. I rolled all of the windows down, Bear liked to hold his arm out the window in the wind.

The next day, Bear and I got up and drove to Deb's house. I helped her cook, and poured us both a cup of coffee. We fed the kids, and let them play in the other room, while we caught up and *fixed everything that was wrong with the world!*

We finished up the dishes and grabbed another cup of coffee. Deb got out some pictures of her daughter and the rest of the family. We had always felt comfortable with each other. Our mothers had become friends while we were in school. I had known Deb since the third grade.

About noon, Stevie Bear and I got ready to go home. I had to work a special dinner being held at the Country Club that evening. I thanked Deb for the breakfast and the hospitality.

"We'll do it again sometime soon! The kids have so much fun together!"

We drove home.

WHO WAS THAT GRAY-HAIRED MAN?

I got ready and drove to work. For some reason the manager wasn't working. I asked where she was. *"She's sick!"* replied Joe.

The air was *thick* though. There was a *strange feeling* at work all night, *like someone had died,* or something. No one was laughing like usual. *I really had no idea* what was going on. I worked through the dinner, cleaned up everything and went home.

Momma and I attended church above a bookstore, The Christian Bookshelf, in Herrin. The rest of the family attended different churches in the area. After church, we all would go to Mom and Dad's house and have lunch. Today, we decided to stop by KFC for a bucket of chicken and the fixings. After losing Ma Ripley this week, nobody felt much like cooking.

After lunch, we took Stevie to play at the park. While Stevie was swinging, Mom and I sat at the nearby picnic table and talked.

"I've been thinking about something. I just may go over there in the morning and check it out that job. If I don't want to work there, I'll just leave. I'm not locked in to anything yet, and it really would be nice to have insurance for me and Stevie."

Mom just smiled, *"It sounds like you would like it better there, than where you are now! You know I don't like it, that you're working at that Country Club!"*

"I know, Mom, but I like working there! I just don't like it that I have to serve booze! I make really great tips! In fact, I have to be there in about an hour. I had better get ready! It's just temporary, until I can find something better! Come 'on Stevie, let's go home!"

He was having fun on the sliding board and swings. We walked the two blocks back home. I got ready and drove to work.

The place was busier than normal that afternoon. I had waited on about ten tables, when one of the older guys, Richard, asked me to come to the office.

"I've been thinking about you. You are divorced and just have one little boy, right? How would you like your own apartment and a new car to drive?"

I just stood there.

"How could I do that? I don't make enough money for a new car and an apartment yet."

I thought maybe I was getting a raise. He walked closer to me, then put his hand on my arm. He tried to put his arm around me, but I quickly moved away.

"I'll take care of you. I'll put you on salary, get you a nice apartment, and buy you a new car. I'll pay all of your bills and I'll even buy your groceries, and pay your kid's schooling when he starts, if you'll *take care of me!*"

Ok . . . now I know what he's talking about. I looked into his eyes, and repeated back to him what he'd just told me. "*And all I have to do is take care of you?*"

He shook his head, "*Yes. That's all I'm asking. I'll put you up in a nice apartment and treat you like a queen! I'll even make you the manager here! We need someone since Susan left!*"

"*Well, Richard, I'm really not that type of girl who would even think of doing that! I'm really not sure where you got that idea that I am!*" I took off my apron and threw it at him . . . tips and all. "*I quit!*" I turned and left the office.

"*Do you want more money? I'll give you more money!*" He pleaded.

"*No, Richard, first of all, you're married! Second of all, my parents know you both! And third of all, I'm just not that kind of girl! . . . Not with you, or anyone else! I don't need this or any job that bad!*" I walked out and drove home.

"*God help me! What have I done? Is that all men think about women?*"

I got up bright and early the next morning, got dressed and showed up at 8:00 a.m. at the new store. I walked in as everyone was lining up in the middle of the main aisle.

The manager asked me my name. I told him.

"*You're not on my list! Who hired you?*"

"A little gray-haired man in a gray suit at the Unemployment Office, last week."

He laughed, "Ok. I'll check it out later. What department are you wanting?"

"I'll work wherever you need me. I can work anywhere."

"All the associates are assigned already. The only place I have open is manager over the stockroom. You probably wouldn't want that!'

"Stockroom? Sure! Why not?"

They were still in *setup mode* . . . putting together the shelving and stocking the shelves as the trucks came in. We had preprinted diagrams, that showed us where to apply product name and price stickers to the shelves. It took about two weeks to get everything set up and for everyone to be trained in their specific areas. I was appointed manager over the stockroom. I learned very quickly how to unload trucks and sort everything, mark it, and wheel it out onto the floor to its respective department. I loved being busy all the time. I memorized all of the departments, all of the prices, and exactly where each item went on the shelves. We closed at nine, but I would always volunteer, when there was any overtime work available.

We worked for about three months, before we had our *Grand Opening.* One day, we got a phone call. The *owner* of Walmart was coming to visit and he was going to be here for our ribbon cutting. We had to get ready for his arrival at our store, the following week. We ordered, cleaned, and straightened *everything* so that it would be perfect!

The ribbon cutting day finally came. We all were busy working, when the door opened and in walked a little lady with a fiddle and a short gentleman in a dark gray suit.

I went up into the office where the manager was sitting. *"There's the guy who hired me that day at the Unemployment Office!"*

The manager laughed, *"Really? He hired you?"*

I had no idea who he was, until that day! *Today, I realized he was the owner of Walmart . . . Mr. Sam Walton! I was personally hired by Mr. Sam Walton! Now there's a story to pass down to my children someday!*

The Manager called all associates to the front of the store. We all gathered around. The lady played a tune on her fiddle. They cut the ribbon and posed for a few pictures. He stayed for about an hour and they left. I laughed out loud as I said, *"I was personally hired by Sam Walton . . . of all people!"*

Many months passed, and I had finally saved enough money to be able to move out of Mom and Dad's house, and into my own small mobile home in Murphysboro. It was just a few blocks from Riverside Park. We walked to the park often to let Stevie play or even fish in the little pond.

After a year, I also had moved from the stockroom to floor manager. I was the manager over Food, Paper Products, Party Supplies, Household, Chemicals, and Office departments. It kept me very busy.

I got a phone call one evening, before we closed. I was asked to travel and do new store setups. I loved traveling, staying in hotels, and eating out in new towns.

Doing the setups seemed enjoyable for me, but I didn't like the time it took me away from Stevie Bear. I like being with my boy.

THE BREAK-UP

I had been dating a guy, Martin, for almost four months, during the time I was working at Walmart. He lived about an hour away from me. We talked for hours upon end every night. We got together every weekend when he was off work, for dinner A couple of times, he took me to a baseball game.

He called me on Saturday, "Hi, Hon, I'm sorry, but I won't be able to take you and Stevie Bear to Giant City for that picnic, tomorrow."

"That's ok. We can do it another time."

"Well, it's more complicated than that," he paused. "I won't be able to see you anymore!"

I sat in silence, trying to hear what he was saying. I was trying not to cry. He was a good friend. I won't say I was in love with him or anything, but with time . . . it could have become more. He was a good friend to me and Bear.

Remember that girl you met at the ballgame? Well . . . she's pregnant, and I'm going to marry her."

"Martin, Do you love her? *You don't want to marry anyone you don't love! Is the baby even yours? We've been seeing each other for almost four months!*"

"No, it probably isn't, but everyone in town knows we dated for so long and even in High School. *I'm marrying her, for her to save face! We live in a small town!*"

"*I'll pray for you. That kind of marriage usually never works out in the long run!*"

"*I know . . . But it's just something I feel like I have to do!*"

"*Well, Martin, you are a good man. I'll be praying that it all works out for you!*"

I hung up the phone. I cried all night that night. I had just lost a really good friend. Only God knows who I truly need in my life right now. I, once again was alone. *No, I was never really alone. I would always have Jesus by my side! I'm a survivor!*

A few months passed, summer was upon us once more. The Walmart store setups were completed. I worked once again, back in our local store.

THE BBQ

One evening, while I was in my bedroom, getting ready for bed, I was reading my Bible for a little while. Stevie had already been tucked into bed.

"Lord, I know Mom and Dad have always told me, "When I was born, You, God, had already created a perfect mate for me, somewhere in the world! And, You, will make sure we will meet! Well, Lord, I chose the first one, and I messed up! I want You to show me who You have picked out for me! That perfect mate that You created specifically for me! I thank You in advance, Amen."

I had been divorced for almost two years by now. I hated living by myself. I despise being alone, when I got home from work, every night. I didn't like playing the role of Stevie's *Mom and Dad*. After my prayers, I drifted off to sleep.

The next day, at lunch time, I was sitting at the table in the breakroom. Donna, one of the girls in the office, came in and sat down at the table too. I had met her a few times, when I dropped off paperwork, but I'd never just sat and talked with her.

I had been holding a Home Interiors book party for the past two weeks. The books were laying on the break table. She was flipping through one of them.

"Hi. How are you doing today?" We chit-chatted a few minutes. "Vi, you aren't dating anyone, are you?"

"No, I'm not. Why?"

"Well, I would like to invite you, and your little boy, over for dinner, Tuesday night. We're going to have a cookout. We live just out of town, and our little boy doesn't have anyone to play with. By the way, I made an order. Do you know when it will be in?"

"I turned it in yesterday. The lady told me to leave the books out for a few more days, to take more orders. I have to pick up my order next week, when the she calls me. I should have everything here by Wednesday, for sure. I'll just bring it all to work. Oh, look, it's time to clock in."

We both jumped up and walked to the time clock. That evening I got the confirmation call, my order would be ready on Tuesday.

So on Tuesday, we clocked out. I had called my Mom to see if she wanted to meet me and ride up to DuQuoin to pick up my order? I was to meet her in a nearby town, where she left her car in the parking lot and rode with me. She said she would go with me. That way she could get her order and her neighbor's too. Donna and I walked to our cars together. As we walked through the foyer, we stopped.

"Are you coming by tonight? We will eat at 7:00."

"I doubt it. I'm tired. I have to pick up Bear at the sitter's, then drive all the way to DuQuoin to get my order. My Mom is riding with me. It will be really late by the time we get back to town." I explained. Surely, she will realize I don't really want to come over.

"It's only 5:00. We won't eat until 7:00. Oh, yeah, by the way . . . I invited my brother too! You'll like him. He is really cute!"

I looked at Donna straight in the eyes, "Please, don't do me any favors!" I laughed. *The last fix-up I had, recently married someone else!"*

I laughed. Now, I knew *why* she had asked me if I was dating anyone! She pulled out a picture holder and showed me his high school graduation picture. No one looks good in those pictures.

"Of course, this was a few years ago."

"How old is he?" I was hoping she wasn't fixing me up with a youngster.

"Oh, he's twenty eight . . . and he's really nice and cute!" she elaborated again.

"I really don't think I'll make it. Maybe another time."

She looked down, as she put his picture back in the holder and put it away.

"Are you sure? We're having chicken!" As if that would change my mind.

"Well, I better go. Mom will be waiting on me. I won't promise anything. I'll tell you what. If I'm not there by 7:15, go ahead and eat without me, because I won't be coming." I turned and walked to my car. I had no intention of going to her house that night. I picked up Stevie, drove to the nearby town, and picked up Momma.

"Hi sweetheart! Hi Stevie Bear!" She gave him a big hug and kiss.

We drove to DuQuoin and found the lady's house, pulled into her driveway, and she loaded up my car. We stopped to get a soda on the way back. I had told Mom about Donna and her cookout invitation.

"*Vi, you should go! You never go anywhere! You need to get out and make friends! Stevie will have someone to play with!*"

"I really don't know her or her son. It's been a long day. I really don't think so. *In fact, I had not planned to going to her house tonight, or any other night, for that matter!*"

Mom just sat quietly for a moment. Then she said adamantly, "*I feel that you need to go!*"

That's when I told her about her inviting her brother. It was a blind date of sorts.

"*Maybe he'll be a nice guy! You need to go! I'm sure you'll have fun, if you do! You deserve some fun!*" she proceeded to encourage me to go.

"*That may be true, but my kind of fun is visiting family, not a bunch of strangers! I told her if I'm not there by 7:15 go ahead and eat without me!*" I laughed a little under my breath.

"*Bear wants to go!*" Mom replied adamantly.

"I want to go where, Grandma?" Stevie asked, upon hearing his name. He has been in the back seat playing with his toys. He wasn't paying any attention to what we were talking about.

"Ok. If Stevie Bear wants to go, we might stop by for just a little while!" Mom got her packages and got out, we hugged and kissed goodbye for now.

Daddy always said *Hard Work was my middle name* . . . I threw myself into my jobs. I spent plenty of time with my family too. My Aunt Katie and Uncle Bud lived in a nice home in town. They were blessed by our presence at least once a week. Stevie learned to swim in their pool. He loved playing with all of their dogs too. Aunt Katie raised Peek-a-poos. Sometimes we'd just run by for lunch, while other times we'd grab fish sandwiches for everyone, watch a movie and stay the evening. Many times, my Dad and Mom came by, the guys played guitar, while we girls sat in the kitchen and chatted way into the early morning.

As I drove back to Murphysboro, I prayed, *"Lord, why do I feel I have to go there tonight? I'm really not interested in "dating" anyone. In fact, I'm kind of afraid of guys and their motives right now. I would like a good friend to go out with, do fun things with, and have dinner once in awhile. I just don't like being alone!"*

I got to the intersection. *Go left and go home . . . or go right and go to Donna's?*

About that time, Bear said, *"Mommy, I'm really hungry!"*

The thought of BBQ chicken on the grill just sounded good, so I turned right. As I turned into the driveway to her mobile home, I realized she lived across the street from Ma Ripley. I got a lump in my throat, as I thought of all the dinners, and stories she had shared with us over the years. I'll never again get to see her face, or feel her big hugs around my shoulders. I will never get to hear her call the chickens to the hen house, or call the kids in to eat. I will never again taste her sweet tea, or the ice cold well water from the crock on the counter. Hot tears rushed once more into my eyes.

"What's wrong, Mommy?" Bear asked as he touched the tears streaming down my face. I grabbed a tissue from my purse, and wiped my face. I quickly freshened up my makeup.

"Here goes nothin'! Come on, Bear!" I got out of the car, walked up the steps, and knocked on the door.

"Come in! The door's open!" Donna called from inside.

I opened the storm door and walked into the living room. Stevie stood behind me, peeking around my leg, at the strangers in the room.

"Hi, have a seat! We are just getting ready to eat!"

I glanced at my watch. 7:15. Right on time.

"I made baked beans, potato salad and green beans. And we have chicken just coming off the grill. Ted will be in in a minute with the chicken!"

I sat down, as Bear stood shyly by my side. I said hello to the guy sitting across the table from us. This must be her brother. About that time, Donna's husband came in the door, carrying a large platter of BBQ chicken, that immediately filled the room with its smoky aroma. He set the platter down on the counter, and found his seat at the head of the table. I immediately recognized him from Herrin High School. I didn't really know him, or his name, but merely knew his face, from riding the bus together. He must have recognized me too, he started asking me about people we knew in high school.

We chatted a few minutes, until Donna called, *"Come and get it!"*

I got up to fix a little plate for Bear. She had set a place on the coffee table in the living room for the boys. We filled our plates and sat down at the table.

From the living room, I heard Stevie say, *"Thank you, Jesus, for this food. Amen!"* I smiled.

I mostly chatted with Ted. (I found out his name). Donna and her brother sat quietly eating. I felt slightly uncomfortable with two people who just sat and didn't interject in our conversation.

Finally I heard Donna say to her brother, "Have you heard from Cindy?"

He sat there a minute, then turned to her and answered, "No. Have you?"

"No." she replied. I had no idea who Cindy was at this point.

We finished our wonderful meal and Donna got up to retrieve a deck of cards. The kids had eaten a few bites and then went into Ted's bedroom to play.

Donna asked, "Want to play *Hearts?"*

Now, I hadn't played *Hearts* in quite a few years, but I'm always up for just about any card game.

"I don't remember how to play. How about an *open hand* to refresh my memory?" I asked.

We played one round open handed. Then I remembered the game rules. I would catch Donna's brother looking at me. I didn't know what she had told him about me, but he clearly wasn't talking to me. I figured, I must not be his *type. That's ok,* I tried to relax and just play the card game. About that time we heard a blood curdling scream from the bedroom. Donna ran to see why her son was upset.

"He's touching my toys!" Little Ted screamed.

"Now, Ted, Stevie wants to play too!" we heard Donna say. She picked up a Sit-N-Spin and brought it into the living room.

"Just take turns!" she said to the boys, as she came back to card game.

I won't say it was a quiet night, as Little Ted was not in the sharing mood at all. Bear finally retreated to the couch, while Little Ted continued to play with his toys.

After about thirty minutes, it was Little Ted's bedtime. Donna went to tuck him in. Bear laid down on the couch and soon went to sleep. We played another round of Hearts.

As we were playing, Donna asked her brother, "Have you seen Mom?"

"No. Have you?"

She looked at him, "No."

I soon came to the conclusion, neither of them were conversationalists. Neither Donna nor her brother spoke to me about much of anything the whole evening. Ted and I chatted occasionally about an incident we'd remember happening, or a teacher we had in school. I hadn't been in touch with anyone since high school. It had been six years since I'd even thought about any of them. I looked down at my watch. It was 11:00.

"I need to go. I'm off tomorrow, but my sister and I are taking Stevie Bear to Rend Lake to go swimming in the morning. I'm meeting her at 6:00, so I'd better get going. Donna and Ted, thank you so much, for inviting us over tonight. I really had a nice time after all. I'm not sure if Little Ted and Bear have anything in common though."

We all laughed. As I stood up to leave, Donna's brother stood up at the same time.

"I have to leave for work at 3:00. I need to go now, too. I'll walk you out." We all exchanged goodbyes.

"I didn't realize it, until tonight, my Grandma lived across the street," I said, fighting back tears.

Donna said, *"Really? The lady in the house, just passed away not long ago. The family had a yard sale. She had some really neat stuff!"*

"I didn't get to go to the yard sale."

"Wait a minute!" Donna turned and went into a back room. She came back with two creamer and sugar sets on trays. *"Here! I bought these at the sale. They don't mean anything to me. She was your Grandma. You can have them!"* she said as she put them into my hands.

"Are you sure? I'll pay you whatever you paid for them!" I felt the tears well up in my eyes once again. I just stood there for a few minutes crying. I missed her so bad.

She put her arms around me for just a moment. *"I'm sure she would have given them to you!"*

"Thank you, so much. I know just where to put them too! I've dusted these so many times when visiting her. Ma was always cleaning something. She'd let me clean her tea cups and what-nots that she kept in her china cabinet. She also had a salt and pepper collection in there. She'd give me a cloth and let me dust them off! I wish I could have gotten a set of those."

"I saw those salt and pepper shakers too, but they were already sold," Donna replied.

About that time, her brother walked over and picked up my sleeping boy and we both headed out the door. It was chilly outside, so I started the car, to warm it up. He laid Bear in his car seat. He was still sound asleep. We walked over to his truck, as he started it, also to warm it up. We both leaned against his truck and started chatting.

Soon, we were talking about everything from school, to fishing, to work. He lifted me up and helped me get in the back of the truck. We sat on the toolbox as we chatted the night away.

I finally said, *"Oh my! It's 3:00! We've been here all night talking!"*

We seemed to have a lot of the same interests. He helped me down from his truck. We said goodnight to each other. He walked me to my car. I waved goodbye.

"I'll call you sometime!" He walked back to his truck.

He waited until I backed up, and allowed me to pull out of the driveway first. I thought it was considerate. I drove about two miles to get back into town. He was behind me. I turned right down a side street, drove past a *church* and stopped at the stop sign. I noticed that he did also. I turned to the left at the end of the block, by the *old skating rink*. He did also. I turned right and went around the *Ice House*. He did also.

By now, I was starting to get worried. I didn't know this guy. I felt like I was being followed. I started to fear for some reason. Maybe I'll drive to the *Police Station! See if he follows me there!* I turned right at the stop sign onto Gartside Street. I drove a few blocks. I turned left. He turned right. I saw him, in my rearview mirror, go down a few blocks, and turn left. *I started laughing! We lived on the same street! He lived on the North end, while I lived on the far South end of the street! What are those odds?* He was just driving home too. He wasn't *following* me at all. It just happened we chose the same path going home. *How ironic!*

I carried Bear into the house, pulled off his socks and shoes, and tucked him into bed.

I started thinking about the evening I had just spent: I really didn't believe I'd ever see Gary again. In fact, I thought he was cute, but someone had cut his hair in a strange way, and he was a little too thin for my liking. He seemed nice enough though. I thought he was interesting and could be a good friend for me.

The dinner was wonderful. The card game was great. The company was . . . let's just say I'm from a big family of *talkers! No one in my family (aunts, uncles, cousins, sisters, brother, parents) has a problem making conversation with friends, relatives, or even strangers!* Tonight, on the other hand, seemed quite *strained* just trying to keep a conversation going, no matter what I said. For example, when I asked Donna or her brother a question, it was answered with a simple *yes or no!* I wasn't used to that type of quietness. *Oh well!* I had a good time, even if I never see him again. In fact, I had a hard time saying his name. He has the same first name as my ex-husband! I really didn't remember his *last name* at all!

THE LAKE

Six a.m. came early. When I got out of bed, I heard Bear in his bedroom playing with his toys. I found my beach bag and packed all the swim necessities in it. I also packed some snacks for Stevie, in case he got hungry. I called to make sure my sister was awake and to tell her we were on our way. We stopped and got something to eat on the way to Rend Lake. I wasn't sure where the lake was, as I hadn't been there before. We usually stayed around Carbondale or Murphysboro lakes when we picnicked or fished. I had never swum in a lake before. We had to stop and ask for directions when we got close. I was positive we had turned down a wrong road, when all of a sudden we saw water. It didn't take long to find the beach.

We grabbed our bags from the car. My sister even thought of bringing a quilt. Good thinking! My sis had also packed sandwiches, chips, and cookies. We sat on the quilt, and enjoyed our lunch. Then after slathering on sunscreen, we all jumped into the water. It was a perfect day, the wind blew across the water making the hot sand on our feet tolerable. The water was cool in areas, while warm in others. We mostly stayed in the shallow water, so Stevie could play and paddle while his feet touched the bottom. We did take turns watching him, so the other could get out in the deeper water, to float or swim for a little while.

The day passed by quickly, and soon it was four o'clock. It was time to head back home. We packed up everything into the car. I laid clean, dry towels on our seats, as to not get them wet, from our swimsuits. I was wearing a new, turquoise two piece swimsuit with red and yellow swirls printed on it. We enjoyed the whole day in the water, swimming, floating and playing in the sand with Stevie.

I started telling my sister about the guy I had met the evening before.

"You need to go out with him. You don't get out enough!"

"Now you are sounding like Mom! I wasn't even going to go to Donna's last night, until Mom insisted I need to get out. Hahaha. I don't know her at all. They are both so quiet. *Even more quiet than Dad!"*

We both laughed. We chatted all the way back to her house. I dropped her off and we headed home.

ITALIAN SPAGHETTI

I turned the radio up and sang all the way back to Murphysboro. As I pulled into town, I turned down Gartside Street. About that time, I realized we both had mild sunburns, even though we had slathered with sunscreen all day long. As we pulled up to one of the stop signs, I decided to turn right.

"Maybe we can find his house, and invite him to dinner tonight." I said to Bear.

"That's a good idea!"

I was planning on making my specialty, Italian spaghetti and meatballs for dinner. I needed to go to IGA and purchase a few things to be able to make it, though. I turned right, and went down to the road, where I remembered he had turned onto last night.

I drove slowly, looking to see if I could recognize his truck. It looked black under the streetlights last night. I remembered also it was a GMC stepside. I saw a truck that I thought might have been his. It was backed under a carport, on the side of the house.

I parked on the side of the street. I told Bear, "Stay in the car, in case it's not his house. I'll be right back." I walked up to the door and knocked.

"Hey, what are you doing here?"

I opened the door and looked up to the interior window. "I'm on my way home from swimming. I thought you might want to come by and eat supper with us tonight, if you haven't eaten yet."

"*No, I haven't yet. What are you making?*"

"*Well, I'm on the way to IGA to get a few things to make my famous Italian spaghetti and meatballs!*"

He was washing dishes. He invited me up the steps.

"Stevie Bear's in the car." I turned around to get him.

We went up the steps and sat on the couch in the living room. He finished up the dishes, and joined us right away.

"Hey, make me a list, and I'll go by Green's and get what you need. Tell me your address and I'll be by there in a few minutes."

He handed me a pen and paper. I made out the list of groceries I needed. We left.

We turned the radio up and we sang all the way home. I went in, and changed into my clothes, as I was still in my bathing suit. I washed Stevie Bear up and changed his clothes. Went in and put the hamburger in the skillet and put on a big pot of water to boil. I turned on the oven to preheat. I got the garlic bread out of the freezer.

It wasn't long until I heard a knock on the door. It was him. I opened the door and helped him with the bags. I pretended to tip him for the delivery. He grinned at the gesture.

He really didn't say a lot, but he seemed to open up more as we talked. I figured out he was more of a *one on one* person, he absolutely *hated* crowds. I unpacked the groceries, made the sauce, and put the noodles on to boil. I made a fresh pot of tea and emptied a couple of ice cube trays into a bowl. He sat quietly with Bear in the living room watching TV, while I finished putting the dinner on the table.

"It's soup!"

They both came in and sat at the table. Bear said the prayer. He finished by saying, *"Thank you Jesus for the spaghetti! Amen!"*

Gary kept complimenting my cooking, while we ate. That was nice to hear, after being single for so long. Of course not too many people would turn down my spaghetti and meatball dinner.

After we finished eating, we moved into the living room, turned on the TV, and watched a couple of shows. Stevie went into his bedroom, to play with his toys. We started talking about everything, who we knew, family, pets, children, every subject we could think of.

At 8:30 I excused myself and drew Stevie's bath water. I washed his back and shampooed his hair. He finished his bath and put his pajamas on. He came into the living room, where we were sitting on the couch.

Stevie stood in front of me, *"Mommy, is he gonna be my new Daddy?"*

I laughed a little, *"I don't know, Bear, but we don't want to scare him off!"*

He gave me a hug and kiss. Then he turned to Gary, and gave him a big hug and a kiss on the cheek too.

Gary stood up. "Mind if I tuck him in?"

"I think he'd like that."

Bear grinned as Gary led him into the bedroom and tucked him into bed.

He soon came back and sat on the sofa beside me. We talked until 3 am. We couldn't believe how quickly the evening had passed. He got up, I followed him to the door, and we told each other goodbye.

The next day after work, he stopped by Walmart and picked me up, then we drove to the sitter, to pick up Bear. We drove back in to town, to get some dinner at one of the local restaurants. We ate a nice meal and went back to my place to watch The Thursday Night Movie, as Bear played in his room. We stayed up until 3:00 a.m. again, telling each other what we'd been through.

On Friday, we went to the ballgame. Gary played fast pitch softball on a local team. I was introduced to the ball players and their girlfriends. I sat on the bench and chatted with the girls as we watched the game. Sometimes, we would all go for pizza after a ballgame on the weekend. After the game, that night, we went back to the house and watched the TV shows. Once more, we stayed up until 3:00 a.m. talking again, about what we'd been through, and we both agreed that we *never, ever, ever,* wanted to get married again!

THAT WAS FAST

A couple of weeks went by, since we had met. Gary and I had become an *item*. We saw each other every evening, after work. We spent all day and evenings together on the weekends. He even let me cut his hair. Now, I guess you are thinking we are holding hands, kissing, and making out, after Bear goes to bed . . . No! We *haven't even held hands* yet! I had made my mind up, that I didn't want any random contact with him, or anyone else, until marriage was a possibility. I had made a promise to myself and to God to be cautious with men. I had been hurt so many times before, when I thought someone truly loved me. I'd let them get closer than I really believed in, or was comfortable with. This time it was going to be different. He was a good friend. I'll admit, I did have fun when we were together though.

One day at work, I was putting up the Hallmark cards on the display. On the other side was a coworker, Maggie, who was also putting up cards.

I said jokingly, *"Maggie!"*

"What, Vi?" she chimed.

"Guess what?"

"I give up, Vi! What?"

"*I'm getting married!*"

"*Really? Who to? That Martin, guy?*"

I laughed, "*Oh no! He's gone! Do you know Donna in the office?*"

"*The quiet one?*"

"*Yes. It's her brother!*"

"*Well, congratulations!*"

"*Just one thing!*"

"*What's that?*"

"*You can't tell anyone!*"

"*Why not?*"

"*Because, he doesn't know it yet!*" I laughed.

"*Oh, you had me going there, for a minute!*" We both laughed as we continued filling the card rack.

Maggie and I went to lunch together that day. I explained about Martin and how we had separated. . Then, I explained how I met Donna's brother.

"*What's his last name?*"

"*You know . . . I don't know . . . We haven't talked about that! There is one problem, though . . . I have trouble calling him by his first name . . . he has the same name as my first husband . . . I'm still angry and hurt from the divorce!*"

She laughed, "*Just call him George!*"

We both laughed so hard that I cried, as we walked back to the store.

That evening, Gary picked me up, we picked up Stevie Bear from the sitter, and went straight to the ballgame. Gary looked over at me, as we were driving through town, *"Oh, by the way, remind me when we get back to your house, I want to ask you something!"*

"Okay, sure!" I said, as we pulled into the schoolyard. We drove around back, to the ball field. Stevie Bear and I went to the bleachers and found a place to sit. The other girls came along, soon after.

We all went for pizza after the game that evening. I was getting familiar with all of his friends. I felt a little uncomfortable around one in particular, though. Maybe she was friends with his ex, I assumed. Oh well, not my problem.

We got home later than normal. I put Bear to bed, as Gary turned on the TV and settled on the couch. We watched the end of a show. I got up to get us each a glass of tea during the commercials. I handed him his glass and sat down on the couch. As I sipped my tea, I remembered what he'd said earlier.

"Oh, yeah, you wanted me to remind you, that you wanted to ask me something, when we got to my house!"

"Well" . . . he set his glass down on the coaster. He turned toward me, reached over and grabbed my hand. He looked me in the eyes.

"I have been thinking . . . *I think I want to spend the rest of my life with you!"*

"Oh sure! If you really mean that, you'll get down on your knees, and ask me again!"

He knelt down on one knee, and held both of my hands.

"I believe I love you, and I want you to be my wife!"

I was shaking inside, all of a sudden. I felt like I was in a dream . . . I just looked at him. All kinds of thoughts rushed through my head. Was he serious? Is this for real? What did he want? I waited just a few minutes, I was holding my breath.

"Yes, I'll be your wife!" I heard the words ring in my ears.

He got back up and sat down closer to me on the sofa. We finished watching the movie.

"I need to go home early tonight. These 3:00 a.m. meetings are killing me!" We laughed.

"Me too! I need a little more sleep, although, I tend to stay up way late into the night, almost *every* night. I read, or sew, or just listen to the radio in my room. Sometimes I just stay up and pray."

We held hands until it was time for him to go home. I walked with him to the door. He stepped down one step, turned around, and kissed me . . . on the right cheek. We waved goodbye.

"See you tomorrow!" He walked to his truck.

Oh, my Gosh! I have a wedding to plan!

WE'RE GETTING MARRIED

We continued to see each other every day, after work. We decided to pay for our own wedding. We set the date one evening, after we had finished dinner. I got the calendar from the desk. We had so much to do. We picked out our matching rings. Our first rings were from Walmart's new jewelry counter.

"I got married in August the first time. I don't want to get married again in that month." I said, looking through the calendar.

Gary looked at the calendar, "I got married in June, so no June wedding for me!"

There were only a few days left in June, so that wasn't an issue to worry about. That would have been pushing it! We settled on Friday, the seventeenth of July for our wedding date. We decided light blue and white as our colors.

The next day, Gary came by, *"The seventeenth isn't going to work for me. Let's look at the calendar again!"*

Friday was still a good evening, so we rescheduled the wedding until the twenty fourth of July.

"That will work! I'll take my vacation, so we can move, after the wedding!" We had already been looking for a bigger house or apartment to move to. My sister and her husband were

moving to Herrin in a few weeks, so we secured their two bedroom house in DeSoto.

We drove to my Mom and Dad's to tell them the news! The house was dark, when we drove into the driveway.

"Oh no! I forgot they were going to North Carolina to visit my sister and her family!"

I got the spare key, and we went in the house. I looked up my sister's phone number, in the Rolodex. I called, and we announced our wedding over the phone.

"Mom, we're engaged! We are getting married on July twenty fourth!"

Mom repeated what I had just said, to my sister and her family. *They all screamed with excitement!*

Mom was crying, *"I told you that night, that you needed to go to that BBQ! I'm so excited! Congratulations! Let me talk to my new son in law!"*

I handed Gary the phone. Mom congratulated him also. She said they were coming back home the next day.

We were waiting in their driveway the next evening when they returned home. Gary helped them carry in their suitcase and bags from the car. We went in to the living room and sat down. Stevie Bear ran to Grandma to hug her neck.

"We missed you so bad!"

Gary and I sat on one of the sofas. Dad made us some coffee. We sat and chatted a minute, when all of a sudden, Gary stood up and walked to my Dad's chair.

"I'd like to do this right, Sir.! May I have the hand of your daughter in marriage?"

Dad sat there a minute, looked Gary straight in the eyes, and said matter-of-factly, *"Son, I gave her away once... and she came back!* This time, promise me, it's *No deposit, No return!"*

We all just stood there listening to what he had just said. Then we all just cracked up laughing. *My dad... The quiet guy... just made a joke! I laughed so hard, I was crying!*

"I'll take that as a Yes!... I promise to keep her and take care of her and Stevie, forever!" Gary piped up, as soon as he could speak again.

We visited until late that night. We all hugged and kissed goodbye. I notice Gary stiffened up, and drew back slightly, when my Mom hugged him and kissed him on the cheek. Gary picked up Stevie Bear, from the couch, and drove us back home.

A WEDDING IN
FOUR WEEKS

I didn't have a white dress, or big, fancy wedding the first time, so these were priority on my list. The girls at work, planned a wedding shower for me.

My close friends and family also gave me a *personal shower*. In fact, they literally felt it necessary to carry me into the bathroom, put me in the shower, and turn the water on . . . just for a second, as they took pictures!

Things just started falling into place. Patti made us a beautiful, three-tier wedding cake. One of my coworkers, made all of the flowers, my bouquet, and the flower girl basket. My family planned the reception, across the street from the church. Our piano player, Gayle, from the church, came in to do the wedding march for us. My art teacher, from Herrin High School, was also a photographer. He volunteered to shoot the wedding pictures. I cut my hair short, and colored it back darker, from the blonde highlights, I was currently sporting. so I would look more natural for my wedding pictures. I did my own hair and makeup. We lined up my best friend, Sheri, and her husband to play the guitar while she sang a song. My sister also sang a song and coordinated the wedding. I had *never been* to a wedding, so I had no clue what to do.

We went to the local card shop, in Murphysboro, to order the invitations.

"When is the wedding?" the man asked.

"In four weeks!"

The man started laughing. *"I'm sorry, Honey, we can't possibly get them printed and back in time, to even mail them out! We can't help you!"*

The next day, at lunchtime, one of my coworkers said, "Vi, I can print your invitations in calligraphy style for you. I have some vellum, too."

I found some blank cards, in light blue, with a white dove on the front. We had our invitations finished in three days. They were beautiful, in spite of the short notice.

I decided to rent my beautiful, white wedding dress, from a local rental place. While I picked out the dress, the owner looked and looked, but couldn't find a veil.

When I went to pick it up, she said, "There's a veil stuffed in the bottom, I found one. Use it if you like."

We chose our bridesmaids, the groomsmen, and my maid of honor.

The guys had to be measured, and fitted for their tuxedos, and shoes at The Tuxedo Company. Gary would wear an all-white tuxedo.

I didn't particularly care for the dresses that The Tuxedo Company had available. I went to the local fabric store, purchased the materials, and made all of the bridesmaids', flower girl, and maid of honor's dresses. I also got material for the ring pillow. Sewing kept me from *totally freaking out,* over getting married next month, to a man that I just recently met.

I prayed, *"Lord, if this isn't you, just slam the doors and close the windows!"* I need this prayer answered *immediately!*

I had a peace come over me, like a warm hug. I knew Gary was *the one* that I was to be with, for the rest of my life!

July twenty second came. Everything was in place. I was finishing the flower girl dress. Gary's little daughter, Tracy, was the flower girl. She had just turned six years old at the end of May. Stevie Bear was to be the *"Ring Bear"* as he called it. He also had just turned six on July eighth. Everything was falling into place perfectly.

THE WEDDING DAY

July twenty fourth finally arrived. It was a long day. I wouldn't let Gary see me before the wedding, so we drove separately to the church.

I met Mom and my sisters at the church door. They led me into a back room, to help me get into my dress and makeup and fix my hair with the veil. *I really disliked the giant bow on top of my head. I'm just not a bow kind of gal . . . but it was a rental, so . . . que sera sera!* All the girls were getting ready. They looked so beautiful in their long gowns of light blue eyelet.

I had my something old, something new, something borrowed, something blue. I was ready. All the hustle and bustle of the evening was coming to an end. The smell of perfume and hairspray.

Gary and the guys were on the other side of the hallway getting dressed. The photographer knocked on the door. He had been making the rounds, to take photos of us all getting ready.

The stage was set: The guitars, the piano, the podium were all ready. The unity candle was in its place. There was a white dove on the back wall behind the podium. Simple, yet elegant with a few flowers and blue and white bows. I could hear the music playing softly, as the people came in and took their seats. I could hear people in the hallway talking, I heard Gary's sister. Many, from the church, couldn't make it to the wedding, because it was the annual weekend at Funk's Farm Campout. They were all gathered there.

My sister came to the door . . . *"We're ready!"* She turned around and took her place with the bride's maids in the hallway.

I heard the music change to a different song.

My sister met her escort and they walked down the aisle. Soon the bridesmaids and their escorts followed. Stevie Bear carried the ring pillow to the front. Tracy walked down the aisle, tossing the white rose petals from her basket, onto the aisle runner. It got very quiet for just a moment.

Daddy was in the hallway waiting for me to take his arm. The piano player began playing *The Wedding March*. The doors opened. There I was, standing in the aisle, in my beautiful, long white, wedding gown, with the long train and the butterfly sleeves. I was wearing a gorgeous pair of white, lacy, high heeled shoes. My veil was attached to my hair, with that big, *ugly* bow on my head! *I held my breath for just a moment.* Everyone stood up, and turned around, as we stood there. Gary turned to look at me, with the biggest grin on his face, that I'd ever seen. My sweet Daddy, squeezed my hand tightly, he walked me slowly down the aisle, as the music played. *My soon to be husband looked amazing!* He stood handsomely, at the head of the room, in his white tuxedo. The bride's maids and groomsmen all standing in their places. There stood Tracy and Stevie Bear in front of them.

Daddy stopped and put my hand gently in Gary's. Gary's eyes *danced,* as he looked into mine. I fought back tears.

"Who gives this woman in marriage?" the preacher asked.

"*Her mother and I do!*" Daddy replied. He turned and took his seat next to Mama, on the front row.

The preacher said the prayer and blessed us. The music played, the songs were sung. The vows were exchanged. We lit the unity candle. Another song was sung. The photographer snapped his pictures. It was all happening so fast.

The preacher announced, "*I now pronounce you husband and wife! You may kiss your bride!*" He bent me over and kissed me long and sensually.

"*I now present to you, Mr. and Mrs. Gary Stearns!*" Everyone stood up and clapped. They greeted us on the sidewalk after more pictures and the signing of the Marriage Certificate.

It was unbelievable! From the time we met . . . only six weeks of knowing this man, and now I am his wife! This was definitely a God thing! I was elated! My rainbow, my dreams are coming true! Stearns, my name is Stearns! I'll have to remember that!

A few more pictures were taken, we signed our papers. *Gary Wayne* Stearns . . . OMG*! He has the same first and middle name as my ex-husband!* God, you sure do have a sense of humor!

Everyone was dismissed, and we walked to the reception hall across the street. The reception was simple, but nice. Punch, cake, nuts and mints. We opened our gifts, and had a bite to eat, and visited with the guests.

Things were winding down, so Gary whispered in my ear, *"You ready to get out of here?"*

"Sure! Anytime you are!"

We kissed the kids and told them goodbye. We had made plans for Grandma and Grandpa to keep Stevie for the weekend. We told everyone goodbye and went down to the truck. Of course the group of friends and family, followed us down to our *decorated* truck too. *JUST MARRIED!* written all over the windows, with white shoe polish. There were streamers taped all over the truck and tin cans tied on the back bumper. We drove all over Herrin. We had an entourage of about fifteen cars and trucks following closely behind us, honking wildly! After driving through town, we headed to Marion, where we got on the Interstate and just started driving South . . . and so did fifteen cars and trucks . . . 75 mph down Rt. 57.

"They are all still behind us! How far are they going to follow us?" Gary asked, as we sped down the highway.

"I don't know! By the way, where are we going?" I leaned over closer to him.

"Well, we didn't really have time to talk about that!" he laughed. *"We only have two days, I figured we'd go where we've never been. I've never been to Paducah, Kentucky!"*

"Really? We used to go there once in awhile for dinner after church. We'd even take a drive down to Tennessee for fish on Sunday. So we'll go down to Paducah tonight and find a hotel."

"That sounds good to me! So, where have you never been?"

"You have never been to Paducah. Well . . . I have never been to the Zoo!"

"Seriously? Where is a zoo? Oh, St Louis! Ok. We'll go to the St Louis Zoo, tomorrow!"

We drove a few more miles. Everyone was *still* driving and honking their horns behind us. They *finally* pulled off the highway and turned around. We were driving in the dark and it was quiet . . . Gary turned the radio up. We crossed the bridge over the river. *Welcome To Kentucky* the sign said. We drove into Paducah. We had no idea where to go. We found something to eat first, then found a hotel, and spent the night.

When we awoke in the morning, I made us a pot of coffee in the room.

"I'll be right back!" He walked out of the door. Gary walked down to the office to get some idea of *something* to do in town. When he came back, I had our coffee cups filled, everything was packed up, and ready to load up in the truck. He grabbed the suitcase and we walked down the staircase, loaded the truck, and drove until we found a gas station. It just happened that there was a group of high school kids holding a car wash there, so we had them wash the shoe polish lettering off of the truck. Gary filled up the tank with gas, and purchased a road map.

We just started driving down the highway. The first place we went, was to Sears, at the Mall. We picked out a beautiful camera with a zoom lens, and a really nice leather case. We purchased some film and a pack of extra batteries. I started taking pictures, as soon as I got back into the truck. We drove to the Land Between the Lakes, went down on the wharf and had breakfast. We gathered a few things from each place we stopped. One thing I collected, was the printed napkins, as well as postcards, from each restaurant we stopped at. I would later place these in a book of mementos. It was a fun, carefree day. We crossed over into Tennessee, where we found a really neat tour of an Indian reservation. After taking the tour, we got a couple of mementos and headed back toward home. We had one more day to spend before Gary had to go back to work. *Home! Home? Where was home now? His house? My house?* After a little discussion, we decided to stay at my house tonight, and drive to St. Louis, in the morning. We will move, in a few days, when I'm on vacation.

We got to the house, things weren't the way we had left them. I had cleaned up the house before the wedding. But, we were in for a big surprise, when we walked into the house! The first thing we noticed that the lights didn't work! We soon learned that someone had been there all day . . . but who? All of the lightbulbs were taken out of the lamps and even the stove light. Gary found them all in a drawer. I decide to heat a can of soup. I opened the cabinets and all of the can good labels were gone . . . not just taken off, but actually gone! I went into the bathroom. I saw Surprise! written on the mirror, with my best lipstick. All of the clean washcloths and towels had been dumped into the bathtub, along with some things from the medicine cabinet. Shaving cream was sprayed all over everything, even the sink and the toilet. Okay, what else are we going to find? When we walked into the bedroom, the sheets had been stripped from the bed. I slept on a half bed. Okay? Where are the sheets? We soon found them under the towels in the tub. My sock and underwear drawers were dumped out into the middle of my bed. What a mess! We cleaned up the place. After opening two cans of pork and beans, and a can of pumpkin, we gave up on the soup idea. I did find the popcorn, so I poured us a glass of tea, and popped a pan of popcorn. We turned on the TV for just long enough to eat our bedtime snack. We snuggled all night on the half bed.

Early the next morning, we were awakened by a rainstorm. The wind was blowing hard. The rain pounding on the roof and against the windows. The thunder was booming and there was lightning all around us. We packed up a bag and headed to Walmart to buy some more film for the camera. In fact, I took my little 9mm camera, so as not to ruin the new one with the moisture.

We drove towards St. Louis, to experience part two of our honeymoon. The clouds hung heavily with water. We drove through the rain and wind. It wasn't a storm anymore, just a gray, cloudy day. The rain had finally stopped, about half way there. We drove all the way to the city, before we stopped for breakfast. We passed the St Louis Arch, looming high above the city, near the Mississippi River. I had never seen such a sight, except in pictures. It was amazing!

After eating, we got back into the truck and headed on toward The St. Louis Zoo. I was so excited to be able to go to the

Zoo! I know most of you can't relate. I dearly love animals . . . large animals, small animals, all of God's creatures. As I was growing up in my parents' home, I rescued, and raised all kinds of animals. I caught guppies in a tin can at the lake, brought them home and put them in a fishbowl. I had my pair of parakeets. I raised ducks and chickens for my Uncle George, every spring of the year. Of course, I had to return them at the end of the year. I always had a rabbit in a cage. I raised baby birds, when the nest was blown out of the pine trees. I even caught a field mouse once. I put him in a shoebox. I had him about a week. I got up one morning and he was just gone! *I have no clue where it went!* I trapped a big, yellow feral cat once. He eventually became a great pet. Of course, I always had a bunch of cats and dogs on the three acres at the motel, where we lived. *I took care of them all!*

We pulled into the Zoo parking lot. We were shown where to park by an attendant. We walked under the big arch at the entrance. I felt like Dorothy entering The Land of Oz. We walked and took so many pictures of all the animals. We stayed the better part of the day just walking and trying to see it all. We decided to head back to the truck and drive back home. What an adventure we had packed into the two short days that we called our honeymoon.

I was off for two weeks of vacation, but Gary had to go back to work the next morning.

So much changed during the next few weeks. We moved into a larger, two-bedroom place, in a nearby town. I quit my job at

Walmart, due to the fact I had a family member working there, now. I was a sister-in-law to Donna now. Walmart had a company policy in place at that time: No family members were allowed to work together, within the company. She was expecting a baby and needed the insurance, so I gave up my job. I went to work in a restaurant for a while, then found a job as an apartment manager in Carbondale, working for a friend of my parents. A few months later, I was hired in direct sales at a local weight loss company that had come to town. Gary continued working for his Dad in construction.

We continued to attend The Christian Bookshelf, the church we had gotten married in. The church attendance was growing rapidly. Our senior pastor had recently passed away, so we were looking for a new pastor, as well as a new building. We eventually purchased an old club building and some land just north of town. Gary helped remodel all of the buildings and soon, we were moved into a much larger, beautiful church. The church body voted to rename the church Christian Life Center, because The Christian Bookshelf just didn't fit anymore.

We went to a healing conference at our church. Jerry Savelle was the visiting evangelist. Gary's seventeen year old cousin, Marcy, had been diagnosed with cancer. We invited her and her family to go along with us, so that she could be prayed for. There were about 20 family members there, in that evening service. Many miracles were happening all around us, as the man of God prayed for headaches, back pain, foot pain, and stomach pain, as well as other ailments.

Then he scanned the room and asked, "Is there anyone here, who is believing for a child, and can't seem to conceive?"

I was in my chair, fervently praying for our young cousin to be healed of cancer.

I had three people around me say, *"That's you, Vi. Stand up!"*

"No! We are not here for me! We are here for Marcy!" I sat firmly in my seat. I was now being poked as they insisted I stand up anyway.

"Well, ok. But I didn't come here, tonight, for me!"

I reluctantly stood up. I looked at the evangelist.

He held his hand toward the congregation, as he prayed, "Lord, I pray for these women standing in Faith, that their wombs will be opened, and they will all be able to conceive a child!"

He went on and prayed for many more symptoms, even marriages to be healed. No one laid hands on us, we all just stood up. He prayed for us, as he waved his right hand back and forth, across the congregation. I actually fell back into my chair, as he waved his hand toward me.

I heard a quiet voice say to me, *"You will conceive a child soon!"*

That was an experience I'll never forget! My idea for having children was to have them early, when we were young, then when they were out of the house, we would still be young enough to enjoy the grandkids. That was *my* thinking. In fact, before Gary and I got married, we looked at a houseboat. We made plans that day, to retire at forty, and live on a houseboat.

I told him, "Well, since we won't be having any more children, we can retire early and live on a houseboat and fish all day. We agreed on that plan.

"It'll be ok. You have one and I have one. That'll be enough kids!"

We got word a short time later, that Gary's cousin, Marcy, had lost her fight with cancer, and passed away. That was the first time I had ever been to the funeral for a teenager. My heart went out to our aunt and uncle, our cousins, as well as everyone else in our family. It was such a sad time for all of us.

GOOD NEWS/BAD NEWS

Every day, I got a horrible headache. I would take a Tylenol and lay down on the couch. I had to cover my eyes, as the light made it hurt worse. I'd finally drift off to sleep. After a couple of hours, the pain would ease up, and I could continue with my day. I went to work at one o'clock, so that usually worked out ok. I called the local clinic, when as I realized I was having *migraine headaches*. I went in to the clinic, and Dr. Rogers prescribed me a medication to help ease the pain.

One Monday morning, I awoke to a strange piercing pain in my left side. I went ahead and went to work. It was hard to concentrate on sales that day. As the day progressed, the pain got worse. I went home early. I was 28 years old! What could it possibly be? Appendicitis?

Early the next morning, I called Dr. Rogers. She said to come in, as soon as possible, and she would work me in. It was a few miles to get to the clinic, so I got ready, and left the house right away. Upon arriving at the doctor's office, I checked in, and the nurse sent me to the lab to get blood drawn and a urine test. I was then sent next door, to the hospital, to have a Doppler Ultrasound. The technician doing the test was quiet during the whole procedure. I was in so much pain. I thought for sure I was having an appendicitis attack. I was sent back to the clinic afterward. It seemed like it took forever for them to call my name. I finally was called back to see Dr. Rogers. She took me into her office.

"Have a seat, Vi." she said pointing to a chair. I walked over and sat down. I was still trying not to cry, due to the pain in my side. *"Well, I have good news and bad news!"*

"Give me the good news first, so I can handle the bad news," I quipped.

"Well, the good news is . . . after all these years . . ." She hesitated. *"You are pregnant!"*

I just sat there in disbelief, to put it mildly. She looked down, put her hand on my arm, and continued, *"The bad news is . . . it's in the tube!"*

My mind raced one hundred miles an hour at that time. *What did that mean? I had heard of it, but never knew what it really meant!*

"That's your pain! If we don't do something quickly, it will burst and you will have to have surgery!" She said, choosing her words carefully.

My elation quickly became tears once more. I shook uncontrollably, as Dr. Rogers just stood there. Shock . . . She grabbed a washcloth, wet it, and put it on my face, as I reeled my emotions back in.

She tried to console me, *"I'm so sorry, I know you're in a wonderful marriage! I don't know why it had to happen to you! You have waited for so long to have a baby!"*

I just sat there, trying to digest what I had just heard. The doctor left the room. Soon a nurse came in and handed me a bottle with a few pills in it.

"Take one a day, for three days. Then come back on Thursday, for another ultrasound. I'm so sorry," she said, as she exited the room. At the door, she turned around, "We will see you Thursday, at nine a.m."

I picked up my purse and quietly left the clinic, and drove straight home. I called my Mom and told her what the doctor had said.

"*But, Vi . . . now you know you can get pregnant, and remember what God told you!*"

"*Yes, He promised me a baby!*" I did remember what He had said.

My family was astonished that I had even conceived a baby, but now, I was going to lose it.

"*God, I don't understand! Why would you promise me a child, and then allow this to happen?*" I cried, as I took the first pill and swallowed it with a little water. My husband wouldn't be home for a while, so I laid down on the bed to rest.

The days passed slowly, that week. Thursday morning finally came. As I slowly got dressed, I wondered to myself, what he or she would have looked like? I held back the tears. I drove to the clinic. They immediately sent me to the hospital. I put on my gown and laid back on the table. Soon the technician came in. It was the same young girl who had been there on Monday. This time she greeted me warmly, and chatted with me, as she moved the Doppler over my abdomen. She stopped to take a couple of pictures. Suddenly, she quit talking in mid-sentence . . . *"Oh, My God!"* she said aloud. She stood up, dropped the Doppler on the table, and ran out of the room. I just laid there . . . minutes passed . . . *"I Have To Pee Now! Really Badly! What in the world was wrong now?"* I screamed. No one heard me. About an eternity went by . . . then the door opened and the technician and the doctor entered the room. They both walked over to the machine and just stared at the screen.

"Look!" she stared at the screen, *"Right there!"*

"Yes! *I have never seen that before*!" Then there was a long silence . . .

"I looked up and was able to squeak out, *"I have to pee . . . My eyes are yellow!"* I was trying to get my mind off of the silence and my overly full bladder.

They both looked down at me and Dr. Rogers said, *"Oh, I'm sorry! You've been there awhile! The bathroom is just down the hall on your left!"*

When I arrived back in the room, Dr. Rogers was gone. I was instructed to get dressed, and meet her back in her office for the results. I was expecting to be told the baby is gone now. At least the *pain* was gone! That was a relief to me. (And I got to expel my bladder, so I was feeling pretty good.) I got dressed and left.

"We can always just start over! Lord, You promised me a baby!" I cried out loud, as I drove back to the clinic.

THE MIRACLE

The nurse was waiting for me, as I entered the clinic door. "Come on back, Mrs. Stearns", she said, as she turned to walk down the hallway.

Once again, I found myself in Dr. Rogers' small office. But this time, she was sitting at her desk. She turned around, I saw a puzzling grin on her face.

"Well, I guess you really did get your miracle, Vi!"

"What do you mean?"

"The baby moved down, out of the tube. *But it's the strangest thing I've ever seen. It has reattached near the mouth of the womb!"*

"What?" There were those tears again! This time they were *happy tears*!

"Yes, you are going to have a baby!" She came over and hugged me, as she wiped away tears of her own. She told me to go to the front desk and make another appointment for next month.

I just stood there, once again, gathering my bearings.

The week from Hell, filled with wondering and worrying, had just turned around and became a wonderful week after all!

I praised the Lord all the way home! I couldn't wait to call *Grandma and Grandpa* to tell them the good news!

Daddy and Momma were so excited to hear the amazing miracle that God had done!

I continued to have migraine headaches every day. I had developed acne all over my face, all of a sudden. *I didn't have acne when I was a teenager! I had a sudden, all day long hot flash! I was totally miserable at work. I developed chronic allergies, infections, and even gestational diabetes. I even continued to have a period every month, which was unexplainable, even for the doctor, and was very unnecessary, the way I looked at it!*

I was at the clinic for checkups every week, for a month, to make sure everything was going as normal.

The doctor said, *"Vi, you're just pregnant, but your body acts like you're dying!"*

Of course, there was *nothing they could give me* while I was pregnant. She did, however, put me on a diabetic diet. I muddled through the weeks and months, as I tried my best to get through work. I was constantly nauseated, but I only gained thirteen pounds throughout the whole pregnancy. I was admitted into the hospital a few times with early hard, labor pains, but was soon was sent home when they subsided. I had such a terrible time getting pregnant with the baby. There are *nine years* between my children. I also suffered so many severe complications, during the pregnancy. On Friday, August thirty first, I was admitted into the hospital. Dr. Rogers cancelled her appointments for that day, and sat by my bedside, until I went into the labor room. After three days on IVs of Pitocin, Dr. Rogers said, *"The baby is in distress! We must do a C-section!"*

I was so tired and extremely hungry. It had also been three days since I had eaten a bite of food. I don't heal well from any type of cut, so the thought of being cut open to deliver my baby scared me terribly. My blood pressure went sky high, therefore, preventing the C-section. We had so many people praying for me, that our baby would be born easily, and in good health.

After a long, hard, natural labor, three days later, on September second, Labor Day, I finally delivered our little miracle. She was born *twenty one days after her due date!* When she was finally born, the umbilical cord had to be cut prior to the delivery of her shoulders.

Doc looked at me and said, *"We'd better put off tying your tubes today, as she may be a candidate for crib death! The cord was wrapped tightly around her neck five times! I'm sure that you and your husband will probably want to try for another one, if something happens to her. Vi, she is beautiful! Do you have a name for her?"*

I had about three seconds to reply, *"Yes. For sure! We would want to try again! Yes, her name is Toni Michelle!"*

While in the hospital, I questioned if I had made the right decision. The next morning before being released from the hospital, Dr. Rogers suggested we wait for six months, then she will tie my tubes. I was actually *visibly* bruised, black and blue all around my waist. We definitely did not want any more children in our lives. We were both getting older now.

SHE'S DEAF

We were discharged from the Hospital. On the way home, we passed the Mall.

"Let's stop and have the baby photographed!" I said.

We stopped at the Mall, went into Sears, and had some of the most beautiful pictures taken. Toni was so cooperative, she even smiled! Then we went home with our beautiful baby girl.

A few days passed and I got a knock on the door. It was a lady from the Health Clinic. We check on all newborns in the county, to make sure they are thriving. She walked across the living room floor, where she saw Toni peacefully sleeping in her port-a-crib.

She looked closely at her and then turned around looked at me, "She is a beautiful baby, but I feel so sorry for you!"

"Sorry? Why? What are you saying sorry for?"

"Well, I'm going to make you an appointment as soon as possible. She is obviously stone deaf! Here's my card. I'll call you when I get back to the office with your appointment. It will be a hard road for you. Again, I am so sorry!" as she walked toward the door.

"No, she isn't! Why would you say such a thing?"

"It's obvious! She has whitish rims in her ears. *She is stone deaf!*" She patted me on the arm, and left.

"*Stone deaf! Stone deaf? Lord why would you answer my prayers after all of these years? And now she's stone deaf!*" I cried out to God.

I looked it up in the encyclopedia. I read, "A petrified eardrum. Deaf and dumb."

"*I trust You, Lord!*" I prayed for my daughter. As I prayed, she woke up and looked at me. My beautiful little girl. God had answered a prayer, of many years. "*What now Lord?*"

I gently snapped my fingers to the right of her face. *She jerked her head suddenly to the right.* I snapped my fingers to the left side of her face. *She jerked her head to the left.* I clapped my hands loudly in front of her face. *She jumped!*

I heard a soft voice say, "*She's not deaf. She's a miracle!*"

"*That's right! You are not deaf, my baby Toni Michelle! You're my Miracle!*" I said aloud.

Toni closed her eyes and went back to her peaceful sleep. It was hard to believe what I'd heard that morning. *In fact I didn't believe it at all! As the day went on, I found it harder and harder to even think about!* Of course, I called my Mom and told her what the nurse had said.

Momma said, "God will take care of it whatever it is! He knows what you can handle."

"*Handle? What I can handle? I just lived through close to 10 hellacious years of being told I couldn't have any more children! And when I did get pregnant, I almost lost her!*" I cried!

The day came when I took Toni to the ENT Specialist to have her ears tested.

He did all of the tests, looked in her ears, looked sternly at me and said, *"Her ears don't timbrel. That means her eardrums don't move!"* He hesitated. *"Not at all! But . . . um . . . it's strange, because she seemed to be able to hear me, when I called her name! I've never seen this before! Her eardrums don't move at all! The ability to hear is all dependent on the eardrums moving, when the sound hits them! When they don't move, the child is in fact deaf! Hers actually are abnormally convex! The normal eardrum is concave! I suggest you bring her back next year when she's older, and we will check her ears again!"*

We left the office, got in the car and praised the Lord. *Even the specialist was mesmerized! He knew she could hear, even though all signs and symptoms she portrayed, said it was impossible!*

"With God, All Things Are Possible! I praise You, Lord and thank You, Lord, for confusing the doctor, and for healing my daughter, Toni's, ears!" I praised Him all the way home.

A NEW LAND

Soon after having Toni, Gary was *laid off* for the winter. He was a carpenter. Because of the weather, in Southern Illinois, being so icy, cold and wet, construction came to a halt, in September. Gary would start in September saying, "We have to get ready for winter . . . *No jobs!*" He would say that almost every day. I believe in all the time I knew him, that was his only *real fear* in life. He was a family man. As I said before, he was a very quiet person, in a crowd of three. I love him with all of my heart, and wouldn't do anything to upset him. Working and providing for his family, were his number one goal in his life. He feared September every year, as jobs would get scarcer and scarcer.

In early summer of 1985, over six months had passed, Toni was doing very well. She was alert and eating well. Her neck finally healed up from the marks left by the umbilical cord being wrapped around it. She was a fine, healthy, happy baby.

I went in to the clinic for my pre-op tests, for my tubes to be tied. I had blood drawn, as well as urine tests, and the usual. I was called to the front desk.

The nurse took me aside, *"Well Vi, Dr. Rogers won't be able to do your surgery tomorrow!"*

"Why not? Is she delivering a baby?"

She looked me in the eye and laughed, *"She sure is! Yours, in about 6 months!"*

Well . . . You could have blown me over with a feather!

"No! You're kidding! Right? We really weren't planning any more children! Are you sure? Maybe it's someone else's test results! Please do the test again! This can't be happening to me! I am on the Pill!"

She laughed," *I know! You take it before your feet hit the floor in the morning! That's how I take mine every day, so I don't forget! You taught me that one!"*

I did make them run the test one more time, just to be sure. Yes, it was *positive* too! I also stopped at Walmart and bought two home pregnancy tests, on the way home.

"Someone doesn't know I've already had my baby after all of these years! *There must still be people across the country that continually praying for me to have a baby!"* I cried.

"Okay, God! I just wanted one not two!" I cried. *"We don't even have the hospital bill paid yet from having Toni! Gary isn't back to work yet! Lord, what will we do now?"* I prayed.

I drove home, went in and threw myself across our king size waterbed. My body ached as I started shaking violently! *I was in shock!* I tried to figure out how I was going to tell my husband when he came home from work! Steve came in from school, I told him to go to the neighbor's house and have Mary keep him and baby Toni, just for a little while, so I could rest. He hugged me and left. I took one of the pregnancy tests out of the box. I waited . . . It was positive. I'll wait and do the other one tomorrow morning. Gary came home. I called Mary and we went to get the kids.

We lived in a trailer park at the time. We were looking for land to buy. We were planning to live in the mobile home until we were able to build a house. We found a few acres just down the road. The day we went to meet with the owner, he told us we couldn't move our mobile home there. It was zoned, no mobile homes, so we signed a month by month lease on the lot, in the park, where we currently lived.

In June, my Mom called me early one morning.

"Vi, do you have today's paper?" Mom was excited.

"Yes, right here. I'm reading it, while I'm drinking my coffee."

"Look in the want ads. Down on the right, under Property for Sale, there's an ad for fifteen acres."

"Wow! There's no way we can afford fifteen acres! Do you know what acreage is going for right now? It's high! We just tried to buy seven acres down the road here!"

"Just call them. I'll wait. Call me back. Maybe they still have it. I'll go with you to see it, if you want to!"

I called. The woman said her husband agreed to meet us at 1:00. I called Mom back.

"Can you go there with me at 1:00? I'll come by and pick you up. It's about half way between our houses. I've never been down that road though. I hung up the phone and changed the baby. I was off from work that day, so I wasn't in a rush. I'll go see it, then if it's in a nice place, I'll have Gary go see it also. That was the plan.

I went to Mom's at noon, so she could play with the baby a few minutes, before we met with the guy. We drove a few minutes to see the land. It was filled with hundreds of trees. Mostly about six feet tall or so, but as we looked further back, there were tall trees wrapping around two sides of the property. It was about ten minutes to the middle of town, ten minutes to Mom's house, and ten minutes to Herrin, where my sister and her husband had moved. It seemed to be perfect place to build a house. When the owner said we could buy it for contract for deed, I was ecstatic! I took Mom home, and we visited until Gary got off work. We met him later at the land. We signed the papers the next day and paid a deposit. Our plans were the same, to move the mobile home onto the land, live there until we could build a house, and then sell the mobile home.

It took a couple of weeks to dig a lagoon, get the water tap in, and get the electrical pole set in. We called a friend, Mr. Smith, to move our mobile home to our land. It was a new chapter in the Stearns' life. We were land owners! We had fifteen acres!

That weekend, we chose a few trees to keep in the front yard. Gary and his Dad started leveling off the ground and preparing the lot for the new home to be pulled in. It was quite an ordeal. I called and got the electricity run, the water had to be tapped in, and water lines laid in the ground from the tap, the rock had to be delivered, spread, and leveled for the driveway.

Gary, a few friends, and a couple of family members started digging and leveling the ground for the driveway to be put in first. Then the land was leveled for the house. I called the place to have the septic tank delivered and set in. Then, the lagoon was dug to a specific dimension. And last, but not least, we had to plant new grass seed all over the front yard.

We had to call the telephone company to have a new phone line installed. They said since we were the last people in the county, we were also the last on that road, we had to have a *special* phone line dug, because the phone line didn't go down that far. So in order for us to have service, we had to have a dedicated line, which we paid dearly for. The cost was added to our bill, which raised it by *thirty dollars per month for many years!*

Everything was falling into place. All of the paperwork, and the permits were signed. We even had to cut back some branches on the road, that stuck out too far. Things were lining up with the movers. We had a date ready. We were able to cross off everything, which was on our list *of things to do before moving.*

Of course, we also had to choreograph everything at the old place too, and have things disconnected there on the date we chose to move. As the moving day drew nearer, we were in fall by now, and the rains came down. In fact, it rained so much that we had mud up to our knees at one point. Then the winds came. Blustery winds, that practically blew me away, when I'd get out of the car. But we persevered, and it was soon to be over except moving the mobile home and hooking it up.

"Thank you Lord, for answering our prayers. We have a home, land of our own, two healthy children, a new baby girl, and one on the way. Our family will soon be complete!"

THE PAPER ON THE DOOR

We told the landlord at the trailer park, that we were moving out in a few weeks. Our rent there was due on the first of the month. We told him we would move our mobile home on the fifteenth of July, so we needed a two-week extension on our monthly lease. He agreed. We paid him for the extra two weeks right then. Two days later, I came home from work, and there, taped onto the middle of our front door, was an *eviction notice!*

When Gary got home, we went down to his house, and spoke with the landlord. We figured it was put on the door at wrong address.

"Nope! You have to now pay me the full month, or you can't stay, *or* you will have to move at the end of this month!" he said angrily.

"Well, we have already paid you for the extra two weeks! You agreed to it, the other day!" I said as I raised my voice slightly.

"I want you off my land at the end of the month, or I will call the sheriff and have you put in jail!" he screamed at my husband.

We just left. I was already sick from just finding out I was pregnant again. I had such a headache. We went home. Gary was his usual quiet self. He went in the living room and sat down on the sofa.

"What are we going to do now?"

"*Tomorrow, I'm going to call the sheriff myself! I know him, personally! We'll see what he says! I really don't think he can do that to us!*" I walked into the kitchen to make some dinner.

Early the next morning, I called the sheriff's office. I asked to speak with the sheriff.

"He's busy, he can't come to the phone right now," the receptionist said.

"*Tell him it's Vi, and I really need to ask him a question.*"

She put me on hold.

"*Hey stranger! I heard you got married! Congratulations! You still driving that little bomb?*"

"*Thank you! No! We got a bigger car. Yes, I got married five years ago and we have a one year old and I'm expecting again! We just found out recently!*"

"*Well, congratulations again! What can I do for you?*"

"*It's like this . . . We have been living in a trailer park. We recently bought some land and told the landlord we were moving on the fifteenth of next month. We paid him for the extension. Then he turns around, and put an eviction notice on our door two days later!*"

He laughed, *"Hmmmm ... That sounds like Old Mr. Weatherby!"*

"How did you know?"

"We get calls like this, all the time, about him!"

"Seriously, can he do that to us?"

"Well, since he already served your notice, you can legally live there for about nine months to a year, rent free ... if you want stay there! He will file with the courthouse. It takes up to a year for it to go to court. In the meantime, you get to stay there for free!"

"We want to leave, but we would like our deposit back. Our land won't be ready for two more weeks."

"I will personally send him a letter, if you don't get your deposit back. You don't worry about it. He must have someone else wanting to move in on the first. He will try and scare you out of there early!"

"That's good to know. I feel better now. I didn't sleep much last night. *Thank you so much! Have a great day!"*

"You too, you take care of yourself, Vi!" He hung up the phone.

The rest of the month passed quickly, as we finished preparing the land for the move. Over the next two weeks, Mr. Weatherby continued to, daily, put one eviction notice, after another, on our front door. I'd just tear it off, and throw it away. The day we moved, he was on his way down the lane, to plaster another one, on our door. He saw the movers there, backing out our mobile home.

"I'm calling the sheriff!" he yelled at me, as he got closer.

"I already called him!" I yelled back at him. *"Save your paper for someone else!"*

He turned around and walked back to his house, as I got into my car.

The men continued backing out the mobile home. I could tell the truck driver was mad about something!

"It's been raining all night! We don't ever move a house in the rain!" He continued to mumble to himself, as he worked on our mobile home. The last block was loaded. I could see he was still angry, as he walked over and climbed into the cab of his big truck.

I sat in my car and started praying, *"Lord, we've waited all this time. Please, I can't do anything about the rain. We must move today! Mr. Weatherby is already mad at us. Please, we need a miracle today! I thank you in advance. For You, Lord, know just what we need, and are taking care of us!"*

One of the guys walked over to the car, as I rolled the window down.

"Don't pay any attention to him. He didn't want to work today! The other guy was sick, so we called him at the last minute. He'll calm down in a little while." he said. "Me and my wife used to live here. We moved out after five years," he laughed. *"I know that old coot, Weatherby! He evicted us, the day we told him were moving! He's a nut!"*

"Well, that's exactly what he did to us too!"

"Well, Miss Stearns, we are ready to go! You lead the way, we will follow. Take the back roads, where you can, because of heavy traffic and low hanging wires, okay? And be sure to put your flashers on!"

I explained where we were going. He said he knew the area well. He waved and got into the *follow truck*. He was to follow both me, and the mobile home, to the site. I waved as I pulled out in front of the big truck. He followed me, pulling our mobile home, with the other truck following close behind. Just as we pulled out of the driveway, onto the main road, it started pouring rain! I could just imagine what that guy was saying about now! But we kept going . . .

"Thank you, Lord for our new land!" I prayed all the way there, *"Lord, you've got to stop the rain! That man is really mad now!"* It poured and poured as we slowly drove down to the stop sign. We turned right, and continued going down the back road a few miles. Then we turned left. It's a straight shot, from here on out. Up and down the steep hills he pulled the mobile home. He moved over to the left, and took up the whole road, when he could. The rain continued pouring down. We climbed the long hill, on Reed Station road. He had to move the truck over, the traffic coming down the hill was heavy, as people were going in to work. I saw, in the rearview mirror, the trees scrape along the top of the roof, as we passed the long line of cars. We have only a mile more to go, to get to the land. As we neared the three-way stop, the road changed to gravel. We slowed down, as we passed under some more tree branches. Immediately, I notice the rain

had stopped abruptly, in that spot. Almost, as if there had been a boundary line for the rain . . . We came slowly to the three-way stop, as we turned right, the dust blew off of the rock road, as a car came suddenly to a stop, to let us pass. We turned the last corner . . . The rocks were dry as a bone . . . Our driveway was dry, our rock dust swirled, as I drove up the hill. I pulled over as the moving truck slowly pulled our home up the hill and parked. The three guys emerged from the trucks.

The guy that was so mad before, looked at me and said, *"I have never seen anything like this before in my life! It has poured rain, for days, all over Southern Illinois! And we got to a place, back there, and it was suddenly like the water was shut off! It's dry as bone here!"* He reached down in disbelief and picked up a handful of dusty rocks. *"I just can't believe it! I apologize for being mad at you lady!"* He shook his head, dropped the rocks, and went to work setting up our mobile home. The guys were almost finished by the time Gary got off from work. They finished placing the tie-downs in the ground, and then set the air conditioner on its pad. Just then, Gary drove up into the dusty driveway.

"Call it a day! We're finished!" he said as he shook Gary's hand. They got into their trucks and left.

We took Stevie over to Mom and Dad's so he could bathe and be ready for school the next morning.

"We'll pick him up in time for the bus to get him, tomorrow," I told Mom as we left.

We slept in the house that night. I wasn't happy about it, because we didn't have electricity on yet. *Being pregnant was not easy for me, especially since it was hot!*

Needless to say, we had the windows open all night. Gary went right to sleep, but I didn't sleep well at all. I heard all kinds of new noises in the country, that I never heard in the trailer park. I heard crickets, frogs, an owl, and some coyotes howling across the field.

As I laid in the bed, I prayed, "Thank you, Lord for the miracle you showed us all today. You are in charge of the moon, the sun, and the rain," as I drifted off to sleep . . .

UNEMPLOYED AGAIN

Stevie was getting older, and he made friends with the neighbor boys very quickly. The next door neighbor also had a little girl a few months younger than Toni. And we were both pregnant, again. I continued to work at the local diet center in town. Gary was busy with a new house to build and at night he was building a home for his uncle. Mom kept Toni while I worked during the day. I also had a friend's daughter, while she was on summer break from school, watched Toni. I was alone with the children almost every night while I was pregnant. I became very sick as the pregnancy advanced. I had to tell people I was pregnant, because wasn't *showing* yet, and I kept losing weight.

One day, I was called into the office and told I was being cut back to four hours every two weeks. *Really?* From sixty hours per week, to four, every two weeks? That's not what I wanted to hear today! I quit! I was confused! Why? Who would do this? I was told someone had said that wouldn't be able to work now, because I had two babies at home, now. Who would have said that? Now, I had to work more than ever, to pay for these babies. I was told I could draw unemployment.

"Oh, My God! Now what?" I cried. I prayed all the way home.

Gary was working all the time, so that wasn't a problem. I wasn't even *showing* yet. I went to the unemployment office, on Monday morning. The first thing the lady noticed, was that I was sick. I asked directions to the restroom. I disclosed I was expecting in a few months. She said I was not eligible for unemployment.

Weeks passed, as I went door to door applying at every place I found, in the local newspaper. No luck. I walked into the Telephone Company one morning. I asked for an application. They were looking for six new workers. I'd surely get one hired here! The lady wouldn't even give me an application!

She took one look at me, and said curtly, *"Hon, you don't need a job! You need to go home and put your feet up and rest! We couldn't even consider you right now. You would be a liability to us. Come back after you have the baby, and you'll probably get hired. We are always looking for good workers!"*

"Thank you." I smiled at her, but I was crying on the inside.

I went to my Mom's to talk to her. She always had a cup of hot tea for me and a cookie. I also knew we could pray for an answer.

After a short talk, she looked at me, *"Of course you know when God closed one door in your life, he will open another, better one!"*

"Yes! I do know that!" I finished my tea and was leaving the kitchen. Mom got a phone call. It was a friend of ours, looking for someone to upholster some bolsters, for her window seat.

She told the lady, "I can't do them, but my daughter sews. I'm sure she could do them for you." We set a price, and the next day, I was upholstering bolsters.

The summer passed by quickly. The winter was hard that year, with lots of snow and ice. I was in and out of the hospital so much. I was really wondering what I'd have done, had I been working a regular job? I bought an upholstery machine and took a few orders recovering chairs, and a couple of sofas. No jobs for Gary, no food, bills piling up daily. My stress level was way up. I was due on December fifth. It was getting closer and closer to my due date.

"I'll be glad when it's all over!" I'd say almost daily. On Thanksgiving, we went to Gary's Mom's. While I was standing in the kitchen, I doubled over in pain. I was rushed to the hospital.

"You're in hard labor! You aren't very big! You're just a few days early, so that's no problem!" I was admitted to the hospital for ten days. On the tenth day, the doctor ordered a sonogram.

She measured the baby, *"We're changing your due date! You are due on January seventeenth. We want to keep you in the hospital, until then. You are in hard labor for some reason! I'm going to put you on some pills, so you won't continue labor!"*

There was never a day that went by that I wasn't throwing up all day. *Being put in bed was not my idea of spending my days!* Taking pills all day, and waking myself up every 2 hours, all night, to take my pills, was getting old quickly. *I wasn't even showing yet*! I had only gained a few pounds with the last baby. I thought this one was going to be like that also.

"Lord, we don't have maternity insurance!" I cried.

Oh, we did have insurance, but maternity isn't included in that policy. We didn't think we needed it, since *I wasn't supposed to be able to have any more children!*

The doctor agreed to let me go home, as long as I was in bed, and I couldn't lift more than a gallon of milk. I was put on strong muscle relaxers, taken every two hours, until I went into labor.

That meant I couldn't even hold my baby at home. *Toni didn't understand that at all!* Daddy would lay her up against me on a pillow so I could *hold* her.

We struggled through Christmas and the New Year. The older kids would have a nice Christmas at Gary's family Christmas party. I told the kids, we will have *our Christmas* when Daddy gets back to work in the spring. It's what we do now. Our Family Tradition . . . January seventeenth came and went. *No baby yet . . .*

I was still not ready to deliver. So the doctor changed my due date, once more, to February seventh. I saw the doctor every other day, by this time. The other days, I was in the hospital, having stress tests.

"Where are you, Lord? I'm in constant pain now!" I cried out.

My body started swelling all over! Things that worked normally, now didn't work at all! I had trouble sleeping! I had skin problems! I was on the edge of depression!

I was having dreams of the baby being born, and then losing it! In one such dream, I stepped on an elevator with a baby boy in my arms, also hanging on to three large shopping bags and my purse. I was struggling to keep them all. I would set down the bags and rest as we descended, about ten stories, to the bottom floor. I picked up the bags, as the elevator stopped, and the door opened. I stepped off of the elevator, into a large hotel lobby. I, once again, rested by setting down the bags. When I picked them up, I realized I didn't have the baby with me! I panicked! I quickly pushed the elevator button, to find the baby. I rode it all the back to the top floor. But I couldn't find the baby. It was a nightmare! I was wandering around the building. Riding the elevator up and down. Stopping on each floor, asking if anyone has seen a baby, in the blue blanket? I finally woke up. I had been crying in my sleep. Needless to say, that was not a great day for me, but I struggled through it!

It was finally February seventh. Once again, I made my way to the clinic. The doctor took me off of the pills.

"You should be going into labor anytime, now. Call me, when your water breaks."

I drove home once more. It was getting real. There would soon be two babies in our home. One child, less than a year and a half old, and a newborn. It was cold winter. What would we do? We struggled through almost the rest of February. March second, is Gary's birthday. I was swollen up, still throwing up daily, and have now gained almost one hundred pounds, in three and a half months. I didn't look, or feel like myself. *I've never been really overweight!* I was growing sicker by the day.

God knows where we are at all times . . . and He takes care of us all.
God does not forget even one little sparrow. We are chosen vessels to complete His will on earth. Amen.

BAY DOLL

The clinic called, "We haven't heard from you. Are you ok? Doctor Rogers is scheduling your delivery for tomorrow. Be at the hospital at nine a.m."

It's happening . . . it's really happening! I was elated, scared, and confused all at the same time. I went in the bathroom and threw up. *Was I ready? I had to be! We had to be!* I wiped my face and went to lay down.

On Wednesday morning, we got up and Gary took me to the hospital. We are ready to have a baby! They assigned me a room and hooked me up to the Pitocin.

After the doctor checked me, "It's like your body has been in labor for so long, *now,* it thinks you've already had the baby! We will speed up the process. I *know* you are *overdue,* now. We have a new delivery room bed, and *you* will be the first to use it!"

That didn't ease my pain. *Who has back labor with every child? Who? No one! Oh, but I do! Back labor! Hmmm . . . Let me try and explain . . . I've heard "labor is like pulling your bottom lip up over your head." Well, back labor would be like "pulling your bottom lip up over your head and not stopping there . . . keep going, until it reaches your backside!" Excruciating!*

The doctor called the clinic, while she was in my room. *"Cancel all of my appointments for the rest of the week. I'll be at the hospital!"* she said, as she scooted a chair next to my bed.

After two days in labor, on Pitocin, and even after she broke my water, I still had not dilated enough, to have the baby. She, once again had suggested a C-section. My blood pressure rose terribly high. No surgery for me, I'd have to wait it out.

I was finally dilated to ten centimeters. They rushed me into the delivery room. I was crying, as the pain was excruciating. I was *starving* after three days, without food, or water. Just ice chips and lemon swabs, they were my friend. Eight hours passed in the delivery room. No one had slept in the waiting room . . . my parents, sisters, and a few close friends were there. They were all praying for me to have this baby! This delivery was worse physically on me, than the last one! I remember clenching the side bars, on the new delivery room bed, when I'd have a contraction. *The baby is stuck!* I was evidently passing out from exhaustion between contractions.

I screamed at one point, *"Just give me a knife! I'll cut her out myself!"*

Dr. Rogers finally delivered her head, cut the cord, and turned her, but she was till caught on something. Finally she moved down a bit and was born. *The cord was wrapped around her neck three times, around her body twice, and she was holding onto it, for dear life!*

"You have extremely long umbilical cords. The baby could jump rope in there! That's why you had such a hard time in

delivery!" Doc said laughing, "*Vi, we have heard women cursing, during deliveries . . . but you just kept saying "Jesus, Jesus, Jesus!" over and over so fast for hours. And you bent the bars on our new bed!*"

I got back to my room. I cried and thanked Jesus for delivering my baby, safe and sound.

The next morning, as I was taking a walk, around the hospital, I saw Gary and Toni come off the elevator. We walked to the nursery window to see our second little girl, we named her Teri Lynn.

Toni said, *"That's not you-uh baby! That's my Bay Doll!"* And so we called her Bay Doll. I was scheduled to have my tubes tied as soon as I healed up a little. My body had experienced too much trauma for one day. I agreed. I was discharged and we all went home to rest. We all thanked God for our baby girl. Now our family was for sure complete.

The first night at home was uneventful. I was trying to breastfeed Teri, with no luck. She slept all night, so I could rest.

The next morning, though, I was suddenly awakened by a sweet little voice. *"Mommy, Mommy. I got Bay Doll all dwessed up!"*

I opened my eyes, as I looked at my little daughter, Toni, standing by my bed, *holding the baby*. I jumped up and quickly assessed what I was really seeing! I took the baby out of Toni's little arms, and went into the living room. Toni, wasn't even a year and a half old yet! She had *somehow* come into our bed room and gotten the baby out of the crib. She had carried Teri into the living room and placed her on the couch. She then got the diaper bag and took out lotion, a clean diaper, and jammies, and baby wipes.

"*I already gived Bay Doll a baff, Mutho!*" said my big eyed girl, proudly.

Teri just laid in my arms. I checked her over, making sure Toni hadn't dropped her or anything. She was perfectly fine!

"Honey," I looked at Toni. "I really appreciate you helping me with Bay Doll, but you need to leave her in her bed, until Mommy gets up in the morning. Because I want to give her a bath and change her. Ok?" She nodded.

Teri was an identical replica of Toni. We hadn't had time to take a picture of Teri yet. There was a picture of Toni, sitting on the end table that Sears had taken. Everyone thought it was Teri's picture. There would be plenty of time for taking pictures. Being in bed, for the past three and a half months, had really taken a toll on my body. I was way heavier than I had had been before. Even the doctor was mesmerized, because I had trouble keeping *anything* down at all. She just figured it was temporary, and that I'd have no problem losing it, once I was able to get out again. I started a diet program right away. I had to be careful though, I was trying to breastfeed again. Not very well, I might add. I just needed to get myself well and strong again.

"*Lord help me! You've answered my prayers by giving me the desire of my heart! Having a baby after all of these years . . . but evidently someone out there didn't know I'd had her, so they kept praying . . . and now we have two! I am blessed with two little girls, not just one!"* I prayed.

I'LL SLEEP IN THE TRUCK

On the third night, we were awakened, at one o'clock in the morning, to the *strangest* odor. What was it? Where was it coming from? We both got up out of bed. I flipped the light on. Gary checked the heater. Maybe something was on fire? I checked the bathroom. Someone didn't flush the stool? We found nothing out of place! We had no idea where that awful smell was coming from. Gary went back to sleep. It was unlike anything we had ever smelled before. As I settled back in the bed, I noticed little Teri was still sleeping soundly in the port a crib next to our bed. She stirred just a bit. I decided to go ahead and feed and change her diaper before going back to sleep. I noticed she was wet. The whole bed was wet. As I pulled her diaper down. I realized where that odor was coming from. *Oh my, my, my! Never, had I ever, smelled anything like that!* I held my breath for a minute, as I finished pulling the soiled diaper off, from my little Teri. Then I notice what was in her diaper even looked strange. It was hard to explain, it looked like clear, cottage cheese. That's the only way I could compare it to anything. I cleaned her up, changed her diaper, found clean jammies, and put on clean sheets. I swaddled Teri in a fuzzy, warm blanket and fed her as I rocked her back to sleep.

Early the next morning, as I was cooking Gary's breakfast, I was trying to explain what I had seen the night before.

"I'm glad you found out what it was. I was ready to sleep in the truck!' he said jokingly.

I assured him, I would call the doctor, as soon as the clinic was open. He ate his breakfast, grabbed his lunch bucket, kissed me, and left the house.

He was helping to build his aunt and uncle's house. It gave him somewhere to be every day.

I called the doctor, as soon as the clinic opened.

The nurse said, "Bring her in about 11:00. We'll work you in. We've been *dying* to see her, anyways! Doc says she's a beautiful baby, just like her big sister!" I hung up the phone.

I heard Toni waking up, *"Mommy, Mommy! Tum dit me!"*

I went into the living room to the crib. There was my one year old, rubbing her big beautiful bluish, greenish, grayish, brownish eyes. Nobody could figure what color they really were yet. They were huge for her tiny face, with long eyelashes. I picked her up for her morning *snuggle time with Mommy*, before sister got up. I heard the bathroom door close in the other room. Big brother, Steve, was up now, too. He was nine years older than Teri. He was still angry at me, for not having a boy! I told him there wasn't much I could do, to fix it now. I tried twice! It wasn't in God's plan, I guess. He came into the dining room, ate some bacon and eggs, kissed me on the cheek and went out the door.

Steve walked to the neighbor lady's house two doors down. She didn't have children and had kind of *adopted* Steve. Steve went there, almost every day, to help her and her mom and dad around the house. Then, Steve and her dad would fish in the small pond in their yard. Steve loved to fish. Miss Jane would sometimes give him a few dollars when he helped in the garden or pulled weeds and mowed the yard. To tell the truth, he just enjoyed helping people. I called Miss Jane to ask if Steve could stay there, until I got back from the clinic.

"No problem! We just love having him here!"

I got the babies ready to leave. Yes, we had two babies. We didn't want Toni to feel like she had to be *big* now, just because there was another baby was in the house. We also have another daughter from Gary's previous marriage. We didn't get to see her much though . . . maybe someday!

When we got to the clinic, Dr. Rogers checked out Teri.

She said, "She's lost a pound since she's been home. Part of that's normal, but . . . I want to put her on a formula supplement. You may not be able to nurse her enough. I do remember you had trouble with the first one too." I nodded yes. She gave me a sample pack of the formula she wanted her to have.

We stopped at the grocery to buy more. Just what we needed, now, we have to buy formula too! Gary's not working yet. A friend of mine, stopped me in the aisle to see the kids & chat a minute. I was telling her Gary wasn't back to work yet. She saw I had my cart loaded up with formula. She asked me if I had WIC.

"Sure, I do! But it only applies to Toni!"

"Just go down there today and get the baby signed up too. It will pay for all of *her* formula too! Just leave the cart here. I'm going there now, to get Melissa signed up."

We drove to the Health Department, got Teri added to the program, and went back to get her formula. I was so tired by the time we got home. I went ahead and made her a bottle. She didn't like it a bit! Eventually she drank the formula down.

After a week, I noticed her stool wasn't any better. I called the doctor five more times . . . each time, Dr. Rogers changed her formula. It really didn't matter which type, or brand, nothing seemed to be better than the former. She doesn't cry much, but her belly rumbled all the time. I'm not sure, but I think something is wrong with her digestive system. She continues to lose weight. It was almost as if she wasn't getting any nourishment at all!

SHE HAS WHAT?

I had a dream one night that her intestines were only two feet long. I woke up crying.

I picked her up out of her crib, *"Lord, touch little Teri Lynn. We're not sure what's wrong with her, but You know! You know exactly what it is! You made her! You formed her! You gave her to us! Now she's sick! I'm so tired! Please, Lord. I need You now!"* I cried quietly, as I rocked my baby to sleep. I must have dozed in the rocker.

I was still sitting in the rocker when I awoke. Little Teri was awake and looking up at me.

I whispered, "Jesus knows what's wrong, sweetie. He'll tell the doctor . . . just you wait and see."

I changed her and went into the living room where Toni was sitting quietly playing in her crib.

A few days passed, things weren't getting better. Teri was just sleeping all the time. Her tummy was distended and she continued losing weight.

That afternoon, Steve brought home a note from school. *There is head lice going around the school. Please check all of your children today. Call your doctor for treatment.* I read the note and placed it on the refrigerator under a magnet as a reminder for later.

The next morning started out like every other day. After breakfast, Gary left to visit his Dad. He said he'd be back about noon or one o'clock, for lunch. He kissed me goodbye and hugged the babies. He is such a good husband and father. Steve came out of the bedroom, kissed me on the cheek, and left for Miss Jane's house, to help shovel snow off of her sidewalks and driveway.

Gary had already been out blading the snow off of our own driveway. He always drives the truck to town first thing in the morning, then, he calls me and tells me if it's safe to get out with the babies. We only had one four-wheel drive truck. Our other car had front-wheel drive, which was not bad driving in the snow, but not the best. My car actually knew where all of the ditches were, and found them frequently. We tried to keep the gas tank full or at least half full in winter.

Gary always said I was notorious for not knowing where gas stations were located. He'd frequently remind me, "*E does not mean E-nough!*" we'd laugh.

The babies had eaten their breakfast, and I had them down for their morning naps. I sat down with a hot cup of coffee, and for my morning quiet time with Jesus. I prayed daily for others, including my family, friends, and church members. I prayed that the doctor would find out what's wrong with our baby girl. I prayed for God to open the door for Gary to find a steady job with benefits, for the family. Many people we knew, seemed to be sick or out of work, this year. A couple of large companies had closed their doors recently, in our area. Unemployment rate was higher than normal across the US.

I finished my devotional time and washed up the dishes and made the beds. I threw in a load of never-ending laundry. We had a wood burning stove in the house, so I threw another log on the fire. I had lunch ready at noon and gave Teri a bottle of formula.

Gary and Steve would be coming back home soon. I had Toni in her highchair by the time they guys came in the door. They finished lunch and went out to burn the trash. I cleaned up the girls and gave them both their baths before their afternoon naps.

The phone rang on the wall. It was the clinic calling. "Please take Teri to the Carbondale Clinic today for tests. The doctor thinks she knows what Teri's problem is." She gave me their phone number and the appointment time that afternoon.

"What does she think she has?" I asked curiously.

"Well, we won't disclose what we are looking for, unless she gets a positive test result," she replied. I hung up the phone. At least we have time for them to get their naps in, before we leave.

Gary came in the house, carrying an armload of wood, that he had chopped. Steve followed him. We took Toni and Steve to Mom's and told her we were heading for the Carbondale Clinic, for tests, for the baby. She said she would be praying for us, for the doctors to find out what's wrong with our precious little baby. We also prayed, as we drove the thirty minutes, to the clinic.

When we got there, they were waiting for us. They immediately took her into another room and prepped her for some tests. *They actually hooked her arm up to a car battery. I was aghast!*

"What are you doing? Won't that hurt her?" I asked. The nurse assured me it wouldn't and proceeded with the testing.

Teri was just tired and slept through the test. They unhooked her from the battery and taped a piece of gauze and plastic over the area on her arm. Now we wait. We still had no idea what they were testing for. We waited in a small room, while Teri lay sleeping in my arms. The nurse came back in after a couple of hours. She removed the bandage from Teri's tiny arm, and placed it in a clear baggie.

She said, "Wait here. I'll be back in a few minutes, then you may take her and go home." She soon returned and we were released to go. "We'll call you with the test results, after our team of doctors examine the findings." We left the clinic and went back to Mom and Dad's to get the other children.

"We don't really know anything yet," we explained to them. We sat and had a cup of coffee with them as they played with the kids and held the baby.

A week went by, and I still hadn't heard from the clinic with Teri's test results, so I called.

"Oh we didn't find anything. The test was negative," she explained.

"What were you looking for?" I inquired once more.

"It doesn't matter. Her test was negative, so it just doesn't matter," the nurse replied.

We thanked God and praised Him for His goodness.

Teri's symptoms seemed to get worse daily. She continued to gain a half ounce and lose a half ounce. She was always cold, so we kept her in double socks and blankets. She had a new symptom, we could actually feel the formula moving through her tiny body, as she expelled the odorous clear, cottage cheese-like, ominous mounds into her diaper. In fact she passed it so quickly, we started putting oversized diapers on her just to contain it all. My poor little sweetie. She smiled, as I laid her down, into her crib.

Almost a month passed. It was morning ritual as usual. I had put Toni down first for her nap, and was changing Teri into a warm nightgown. Teri always seemed to be cold. She was shaking and so tiny. She shivered, because her tiny body didn't seem to hold body temperature correctly, yet. That's when I noticed there was something in her sparse, dark hair strands.

"Oh no!" I said quietly. She must have head lice!" I said. I remembered the note Steve had brought home from school a few weeks before. I had never seen head lice, so I called the pharmacy and asked "What does it look like? How do I get rid of it?"

The lady explained what I should look for, and if I saw it, just stop by the pharmacy and pick up something to get rid of it. I decided to have Gary get some anyways. I saw white things in the baby's thin fine hair. I didn't see anything running around, but it looked like the nits she had explained. I shampooed all of our hair and sprayed the house down. I kissed Teri's forehead, as I lay her in the crib. My lips were suddenly tingling. I thought it was just the shampoo residue, but it really burnt my lips.

Gary went out to chop wood. Steve was at school, so it was just me and the girls, in the house. I finished up the dishes, and turned on the television set. A black page was rotating on the screen, *IF YOU EVER KISS YOUR CHILD AND IT TASTES SALTY, CALL YOUR DOCTOR IMMEDIATELY!*

Wait! What? Yes! That's what it was! Salt! It burned my lips, like I'd licked a salt block! I jumped up and ran to the phone.

I called the doctor. The nurse answered the phone, "May I help you?"

"Yes, this is Vi Stearns. I know this may sound silly. I don't usually lick my children . . . but I kissed my baby this morning and she burnt my lips! They're still tender." I said, trying not to laugh, because *I couldn't believe I was saying this!*

Immediately, the doctor got on the line.

She said firmly, *"Vi, I want you to take her, immediately, to Carbondale Clinic, where we did that test before. I'll call over there. They will be expecting you."*

I called Gary into the house.

"We need to take Teri back to Carbondale Clinic! I'm afraid they think it's something serious! I actually spoke with the doctor, herself, on the phone! We have to go now!" I told him, as I put on my shoes, grabbed my purse and the diaper bag.

It was a long day for all of us. The doctor finally came out into the waiting room, where we were sitting.

"Come with me," he said, as he led us back into his office. "After careful testing, my colleagues and I have come to the conclusion your daughter has Cystic Fibrosis. We have called St Louis Children's Hospital. They already have all of her paperwork. They will be expecting you at nine o'clock, in the morning. I suggest you drive up there tonight."

"Really? Wait! She has what? Cystic what? Let me write that down! I've never heard of that! Oh, dear God! What does it mean? What does it affect?" I was fighting back burning tears. I was shaking on the inside.

"It's me again, Lord! I know You have this! You know what's best for us. Lord, we don't have even have enough money for a hotel or food!" I prayed when we got into the truck.

I called Mom and Dad and told them what was going on. We made arrangements for them to keep Toni and Steve. Someone had to get him to and from school while we were gone. We counted thirty dollars between us and we had twenty five dollars in the bank for the rest of the week. We had a full tank of gas. We didn't have a choice not to go, even though we really didn't have the money to travel. We didn't know if they would keep her, or if they would just send her back home.

We left, and drove home to pack the diaper bag for a few days. I also packed a small bag for Gary and me. We had never really traveled anywhere, so neither of us owned a suitcase. I did have a small crocheted bag that Momma had made me. I packed it full. We prayed for guidance on the way to the hospital and for a safe trip. We left that night, with a map to help us get to St Louis Children's hospital, without getting lost. Neither of us had been back to St Louis since our honeymoon, so we really weren't familiar with where exactly we were to go.

ST. LOUIS CHILDREN'S HOSPITAL

We parked and found the place we were to take her the next day.

I asked to speak with a nurse. Soon a lady came to the waiting room. We followed her to a room.

She asked, "Do you have money for food and a hotel? We know you had to leave on short notice."

We told her what we had with us. She left and came back with vouchers for free food and hotel that night. If we find we need to keep her, you will receive vouchers each day for as long as you need." She explained. We left the hospital and found the hotel we were to check in to.

First thing in the morning, we drove over to the Children's Hospital. Once again found the room we were to meet Dr. Adams, who would be assigned to Teri. He looked at her, he prescribed her a special formula, and some vitamin drops. He also gave her digestive enzymes that we were to give her after each bottle of formula. Dr. Adams also listened to our questions and concerns. Another nurse came in and showed us how to do postural drainage and chest percussion on Teri to help drain the thick mucus from her little lungs. The main C.F. nurse stayed with us the whole time. She hugged me after the doctor and all of the other staff left the room.

She said, "I know this has to be a big shock to you both. We will give you all kinds of information. Just wait awhile before you read it tonight." She smiled and assured us that Teri was in the best hands. "We are so proud to have Dr. Adams. Just last week, he moved here with all of his team of specialists. He is from the largest Hospitals in Boston. He is making St. Louis Children's the Number 1 Hub of Cystic Fibrosis Specialists in the United States. If you were going to have a child born with Cystic Fibrosis, this is the perfect timing! In fact, Teri is Dr. Adams' first patient to be seen here. You've all had a rough couple of days. Get some dinner and go rest for tonight. Your appointment is scheduled for tomorrow morning. We will have the whole team checking Teri Lynn out."

We thanked her and went downstairs and had our meal in the cafeteria of the hospital. *Our heads were spinning. Just trying to absorb it all. I did read a flyer print out the nurse had given us. Cystic Fibrosis is a disease. It affects the lungs and digestive system of the patients. It is the #1 killer of small children. What? I don't know anyone who has it? How can it be the #1 killer of small children? Those words haunted me all night.*

The next day was a very long day. It was filled with getting familiar with the hospital, the teams, and finding our way around. We met the whole team of C.F. doctors, nurses, and all kinds of lab technicians, x-ray technicians, dieticians, psychologists, a psychiatrist, and a whole lot more. We were shown to the different levels of the hospital and last, but not least wound up at the pharmacy where we would fill all of Teri's prescriptions. Her special diet of Pregestimil (Predigested Protein) Powder was her new formula. Talk about an odor! I almost *lost it* when I opened the first can. That feeling of nausea unfortunately never went away, when I'd open future cans. The Pharmacist filled two huge grocery sacks, full of a myriad of bottles, including her vitamins, formula, antibiotics, enzymes, and inhalants. She was also given a nebulizer machine.

We went back up to the main floor and got our appointment for next month and a parking voucher for free parking while we were there. *I hadn't thought of parking. That would have cost us a pretty penny, the whole time we had been there.*

Gary went down to the parking garage, we met him at the door as he pulled the car up in to the loading zone. We buckled the girls into their car seats, and packed the medicine bags in the back floorboard. We thanked the Lord as we pulled onto Highway 64.

The snow swirled all around our car all the way home. We not only had a long ride home, but we had a long road ahead of us. I looked in my purse.

"Thank you, Lord. We still have the $30.00 between us, as well as the $25.00 in the bank, and a half a tank of gas. Enough to get us home!" I said out loud. Gary just smiled. He knew God was blessing us with each thing we were going through.

"The steps of a righteous man are ordered of the Lord." the scripture came to my mind.

THE EASTER SEALS LADY

It was a hot day in July. Teri was finally putting on a little weight and thriving. Toni and Steve were getting used to the idea of having another baby in the house. I was finally feeling pretty good, after having two pregnancies. The shock of having a child with Cystic Fibrosis had finally worn off. We were in a routine.

I hadn't found work yet, but Gary had worked all spring and summer. He even told me he had possibly a new house to build. That will keep him working all winter long. Yes, things were going quite well.

I went to my Mom's one day to visit. She gave me twenty dollars, and said, *"I know it's your anniversary next week. I want you two to do something special. Go to dinner. I'll watch the kids, if you want to get away for a weekend."*

I hugged her and thanked her. I never asked Mom for anything. I had always made my own way. We stayed awhile and when it was time to go home and make dinner, we left.

That weekend, at church, a couple asked me if I'd like some tickets to the ballgame in St. Louis.

"Really? I've never been to a baseball game there!"

She had them given to her, and just realized they had other plans that day. This weekend was our anniversary week. Another lady heard it was our anniversary and gave us fifty dollars.

"Go to Red Lobster or somewhere really nice on me! Happy Anniversary!"

We started making plans to go to St Louis that weekend, as soon as Gary got off work on Friday at three thirty.

On Monday morning, I was on the phone. One of the ladies at Church had told me to call Easter Seals, maybe the organization could help us pay for Teri's doctor and hospital bills.

I called the number, but the lady I was told to speak to was gone that day.

The secretary said, "I'll give her the message that you called. I'll have her call you back as soon as possible."

I tried calling every day all week. On Friday morning, I had to take Teri to the Clinic for a checkup.

When I got home, I noticed I'd missed a call. Guess who it was from? Yes, it was the Easter Seals lady.

I immediately called back. The secretary recognized my voice. We both chuckled.

"You're not going to like what I'm about to say . . . You just missed her. She left early. She is gone for the weekend. I'll tell her you called!"

"Sure! We've played phone tag all week! I'm beginning to think she's not really there! Hahaha!"

"That's the same thing she said!"

"Well, you have a great weekend!" I hung up the phone.

I have called five different organizations trying to get someone to help us pay Teri's bills. We weren't eligible for most of them, because we made a few more dollars than what they considered within range for their cases. This was my last hope.

We were really looking forward to getting away. My sister and her husband were living in the area near there. They invited us to stay with them while we were there, they lived right next to the race track. They took us to the car races on Saturday. That was fun.

We all went to Red Lobster, on Saturday night, in St Louis. Gary had never eaten seafood of any kind, except fish, until that time. He was introduced to popcorn shrimp, which became his favorite dish! The rest of us enjoyed lobster and crab legs. We went back to their apartment, made popcorn and watched the Saturday Night Movie on TV.

We got up on Sunday morning. Gary wanted to eat before we went to the ballpark. We drove around until we found a familiar chicken restaurant. We ordered and ate our meal. Neither of us had ever been to a ballgame at a major stadium. We were so excited to be able to go. As I ate my meal, I noticed that was getting a headache. Kind of a full feeling and I was having some trouble hearing out of right ear. I soon realized I must have an earache. Just what I needed.

We finished our meal and made our way to Busch Stadium. Gary looked at our seats.

He said, *"We're way up there in the nosebleed section!* He pointed way up at the top of the bleachers.

Great! My head is pounding and I'm on the way up in the clouds. Now, I'm very nearsighted. Sitting way up there, I'll be lucky to even *see* the players on the field. *Oh my gosh!* They really looked so far away. Oh well, it's our anniversary, I won't say anything. Wow! My head was really pounding and I was starting to get dizzy. We finally found our seats. We scooted in just about a foot. I put my purse down on the concrete between my feet and settled in. The players were practicing on the field. Gary and I chatted a minute. I looked around. There weren't many people up as high as we were, but the rest of the seats were pretty much filled up. Gary pointed out the big screens we would be watching the game on. That made it better. There was a lady in our row, about 10 feet away from us. And past her, there was a group of men partying early. In fact, we could tell that they were pretty well drunk already. At least they were far enough away, they wouldn't spill beer on us if they jumped up! Ugh . . . *I can't stand the smell of beer!*

It wasn't long and the first inning started. We all stood, as the girl sang *The National Anthem*. They introduced everyone on the field and the top of the first inning started. My head started pounding harder and soon my ears totally closed up. I thought I was going to throw up. Gary got me a 7-Up, hoping to calm me down. I soon realized, yes, I have a problem with heights too . . . and it was getting ready to present itself more than I wanted to realize. I was trying not to throw up. I knew it was a long way down to the rest rooms. Gary handed me a Rolaids, hoping to calm my stomach, since the 7-Up didn't work. My stomach finally settled down, and the nausea passed. My ear was really hurting and soon I heard something pop and something was running down my neck. I guessed I had fluid trapped behind my ear, and the height we were at must have released it. I grabbed my purse to get a tissue or a napkin, but I had none with me. I felt dizzy all of a sudden and put my head on Gary's shoulder. The lady sitting down from me, must have sensed I need a tissue and scooted down and handed me a handful from her purse.

"Are you ok?" she asked. "I get the feeling you didn't like it way up here."

I answered, "I have ear trouble and I'm dizzy right now. I guess I had some fluid in my ear, it is draining."

"Thanks for the tissue." I said, dabbing my ear. "It's our anniversary and we've never been to a ballgame here. We're here from Southern Illinois."

"Oh me too! I've never been to a game here either. I'm from Marion. It's been a rough week at work. I took off early Friday and decided to treat myself to fun weekend. She paused and then continued, *"I work in an office. I've been trying to get a hold of a lady from Carbondale all week about her little girl!"*

I smiled at her. *"That's funny! I've been trying to get a hold of The Easter Seals Lady all week!"*

She looked at me, *"You wouldn't happen to be Mrs. Stearns would you? I work at the Marion Easter Seals Office!"*

I was in disbelief! *"Miss James? Seriously? I've called you every day, since my friend gave me your name!"*

We both had a good laugh! *This had to be God! Here we were . . . in St Louis . . . at the Cardinals ballgame . . . on the same day . . . sitting next to each other . . . in the nosebleed section! That couldn't be just a coincidence!* She handed me her card. I wrote out my name and number on a piece of paper and handed it to her.

She told me, *"Actually, Easter seals can't help you, but I have a number of a place who can! I'll call you tomorrow, first thing in the morning. I'll give you their number. Right now we should watch this ballgame!"* We all watched the rest of the game. Cardinals won!

After just about an hour, I noticed my ear had drained and I was feeling better. We drove back home after the game was over.

The next day, she did call and gave me the number to another organization I'd never heard of. The man from there called me within the hour and made us an appointment for the next day. We got signed Teri up on their program. They were willing to pay for one hundred percent of all of her bills, from any doctor or hospital, local or in St Louis. They paid for all of her medicines and even picked up some of her prior bills owed. Gary and I could both work. They would even pay for our gas, to and from St Louis, food, and a hotel when we needed it.

"Thank you Lord, for you hear our prayers. You went over and above what we could imagine! You answer us, even when

we think it's impossible in our eyes!" I prayed out loud on the way home.

God had a miracle for us, every time we turned around! He showed us mercy and gave us supernatural favor.

YOU PAID HOW MUCH?

I was coming out of the bedroom after making the bed and cleaning the bathroom. Gary was without work for a couple of weeks. They were getting ready to start a new job. Fall and winter was hard for construction workers in Southern Illinois.

We tend to have harsh winds and rain in fall and then it generally goes into cold winter from November thru March. We can get ice, snow, sleet, rain, and all of the above in layers. Winter is not something we look forward to every year. This particular fall seemed colder than usual already.

Gary said he was going to town, he kissed me, "I won't be long."

I'd had an unusually hard day with the kids. I had been sick, Teri had been sick, and Toni had been suffering with ear problems. Gary knew that entertaining company would bring my spirits up. I was cooking and getting ready to feed the family. Mom and Dad were coming by that evening for dinner. I was making a beef roast with carrots and potatoes. I was also planning a chocolate pie for dessert, and I made two pitchers of tea. This dinner was a favorite of both my dad's and my husband's. I loved to cook, plan, and entertain guests. We lived in a small mobile home, but because we had the purchased fifteen acres, we had a nice place for the kids to play, unlike the trailer park we had moved from. After Teri was born, though, we couldn't afford to build our house that we'd so carefully planned.

We had a little brown and black dog named Bear-Bear. We also had a couple of cats, two rabbits, and we even had a pony for the kids to ride. The kids helped set the table. I checked the baby in her crib. She was awake now, so I put her in her swing in the living room, and wound it up. She was content to swing for hours. Life was good today, so far. About an hour went by and I heard the truck drive up the hill.

"Daddy's home!" I announced to the kids. I went back to the laundry room and took the freshly washed clothes from washer and loaded them into the dryer. I grabbed the folded towels from on top of the dryer and took them to the bathroom and put them away in the shelf. As I was coming out of the bedroom. Gary met me at the door. He had something in his hand behind his back.

"Hi, Hon!" he had a grin on his face. He showed me a little white bag.

"What's this?" I was puzzled.

"It's for you!" He put it in my hands. I slowly slid the box out of the bag, still wondering what it was. On the front of the box it was written in bold lettering, The Holy Bible, KJV. I looked at the beautiful, burgundy leather-bound Bible. It even had the gold edges.

"It's beautiful! But where did you get the money?"

We didn't have money for gifts. Gary wasn't really the sentimental type of guy. He would hand make me a table or a piano bench or a box for my jewelry, but it was difficult for him to buy me a Christmas, or birthday card. I never understood this. My mom and dad were both sentimental, and they bought each other cards, *just because it was Tuesday!* I thought that every husband and wife did that. With Gary, I soon learned that he thought *cards* were overpriced and totally not necessary to give anyone.

He looked at me, "I wrote a check."

I could feel my neck getting hot. Gary did not want to help in the financial department in our household, so I paid the bills. I didn't mind. We were on a strict budget at that time. I hadn't worked in over a year now. Money was tight. Bills were due. I figured he had paid about forty dollars for the Bible. I flipped through the slick, new pages, the price tag fell onto the floor.

"Eighty dollars?" I raised my voice a little bit, "*You paid eighty dollars? Please tell me you didn't! Oh my gosh! That's all the money we had in the bank for bills right now! Take it back! We can't afford it! I can love a ten dollar Bible just as well as an eighty dollar one!*" I was crying by now.

He just looked down into my eyes, held my face gently with his hands and said quietly, "*I'm sorry, I thought you would like it! I looked for so long in the store for just the right one. You are worth an eighty dollar Bible!*"

I just stood there for a moment, looking sincerely into my husband's brown eyes. I realized I had hurt my husband's feelings for the first time since we'd been together. *That's the last thing I ever wanted to do.* I buried my face in his chest.

"I'm so sorry. It's just that I've been praying for extra money to pay the bills this month. We came up way short!"

He hugged me, "How much more do we need?"

"Two hundred and forty more dollars."

Gary laughed, *"It will be okay! You keep the Bible! We didn't have been enough money to pay all the bills anyways!"*

"God will provide all of our needs according to His riches in Heaven!" I said, as we just stood there, holding each other.

I took the beautiful, burgundy bible to the living room and placed it on the coffee table in place of my old, tattered, black Bible that I'd carried for about twenty years.

I continued cooking and soon our home was filled with laughter and the smells of a well-planned dinner. We all gathered at the table, held hands, as my Daddy gave thanks for the food. There was soft music playing in the stereo.

After dinner, we all went into the living room and watched TV for a while.

God knew what I needed to do His will . . . even though I didn't see it at the time . . . He was getting me readied for His service, but I was unaware.

PAID IN FULL

Do you really believe God paid the taxes by finding coins in the fish's mouth? Many I know say that's just a story to make the Bible interesting. I tend to take it more literally, because Jesus owed taxes too.

Gary had been working full time by now. He had been hired by a friend who owned a place that built fireplaces and sold wood burners. We had lived through another winter. The children were growing like weeds. Gary had installed a wood burner to help cut down on the electric bill in the wintertime.

I was getting used to staying home with the babies. I missed the extra money I could make, working outside the home, though. I was getting the bug, you might say. I was good at sales, but most sales jobs in our area were for men, not women, unless I wanted to sell Avon or Tupperware again. That wasn't appealing to me. There wasn't much in the *want ads* in the paper yet. Maybe next year, when spring is in full swing, more jobs will open up and I can find something to do.

I walked down to get the mail. Bills, bills, and more bills. It never ended. I didn't even want to answer the phone anymore. It seemed we were getting behind on everything, the water bill, the electric bill, and the lease on the mobile home. The land payment was always paid on time. We couldn't afford to lose our land. We were buying it Contract for Deed. Another letter from the hospital. We owed *forty two thousand dollars* to the local hospital for having the kids. We were sending *two dollars per week*, and more when we got a few more dollars. *It just seemed like we didn't make enough money!* When we did have extra, we had a higher electric bill, or the car would break down. It was always something taking our money. We could never get ahead! *Forty two thousand dollars* seemed outrageous for a bill, but we had to somehow pay what we could, when we could.

I prayed, *"I am Yours, Lord, God! I give you all of our bills!"* I took the letter, and our other bills, held them up in the air, and offered them all to God. *"It's me again, Lord! We need help here! We can't possibly pay these bills, the way things are going! Gary just doesn't make enough, even working full time! We need a miracle! In Jesus' name. Amen."*

I put the letter in the file box along with the rest of the monthly bills.

Three days passed . . . I had been at the doctor's office that morning. As I walked into the house, I saw the green light flashing on the answering machine. I walked over & hit the Play button, "Hello, this is for Vi or Gary Stearns. This is Mrs. Green. Please call the Billing Department at the Hospital in regards to your hospital bill." I just stood there. What did they want? I'm sure more money. I even had the thought cross my mind, that they wanted to sue us for the balance due. Forty two thousand dollars is a lot of money to owe! I listened to the message again. I slowly dialed the number.

"Hello, I need the Billing Office," I said to the switchboard operator.

"Billing Department. Mrs. Green speaking. May I help you?"

"Hi, Mrs. Green, I'm sorry, I missed your call this morning. I just got back from taking my baby to the doctor's office."

"Yes, Mrs. Stearns, I need you to come by the office to discuss your hospital bill. Can you be here at about 1:00?"

"Sure, I'll be there at 1:00."

I hung up the phone and called Momma.

"Momma, would you be able to watch the kids for awhile? I have to go to the hospital to take care of some kind of paperwork."

"How about I'll ride with you! I'll keep the girls in the waiting room. I need to stop by Kroger anyways."

She drove immediately to my house and we headed to the hospital. I had not disclosed how much we owed with anyone.

"We may be getting sued over the hospital bill."

"Let God have it! He'll take care of it for you!"

"I *gave Him* all of the bills just 3 days ago."

We walked into the hospital and asked for directions to Mrs. Green's office. The lady looked at Mom, *"Ma'am, you can't take the children into the hospital. You'll have to stay in the waiting room!"*

"Oh, I'm not here for me, I'm just watching her children."

The lady pointed me to Mrs. Green's office down the hallway.

"*Lord help me!*" I prayed under my breath. I was lead back to a small desk.

"Have a seat on the stool," she said. "Mrs. Green will be here in just a minute." The young lady turned and left me sitting in front of a computer and a huge file, which was about five inches thick. My name was written in big, red letters on the front of the file. Wow! I really had been in the hospital a lot, over the past couple of years.

Mrs. Green came in, sat on the other stool, and turned on the computer.

"I understand you have a huge bill that you have been paying on. Are you or your husband working?" she asked.

"He is now, but we are so far behind on our bills, from him being unemployed last winter. I'm paying as much as I can on the bill right now." I said, as I hung my head down.

She picked up the huge file. "This is your file. The way you're going, you will never be able to pay it off!" She continued. She opened it up. The top page has the amounts I had paid on the account. "We have taken your account before the board. Your family have been chosen. We had a lady who has recently passed away. She left money to the hospital in her will. Her instructions were to pay off a hospital bill of someone who has a very sick child. I understand your baby girl was born with Cystic Fibrosis."

"Yes." I was holding back tears.

She took a stamp and ink pad out of the drawer and stamped *PAID IN FULL* across the page. I just sat there. Tears were streaming down my face. I didn't care! *Forty two thousand dollars was just wiped away! It is paid in full!* Mrs. Green handed me a tissue.

"We couldn't find a more deserving family to give it to!" she said. *"We see you are trying to pay your bill and just can't. Now you won't have to worry about it anymore! We wish everyone was more like you and your husband."* She smiled.

I couldn't believe my eyes or my ears! Paid In Full! I practically skipped down the hallway to the waiting room. A big burden had just been lifted off our shoulders. I waited until we got to the car, to tell Momma the news. We buckled the girls in the car seats and settled ourselves in the front seat.

"Well, she showed me our bill. *Over forty two thousand dollars was due! We have paid a few hundred on it. It's down to forty two thousand dollars! Mrs. Green told me that we'll never get it paid off!"* I said.

I started crying, as I handed Mom the receipt, Mrs. Green had given me. *"But this says Paid In Full!"* Mom said, *"I don't understand!"*

I told her the story about the lady who had passed away. And in her will she had left money to the hospital to pay someone's bill. Not just anyone . . . *but someone with a sick child.*

"They chose us!" I cried even harder, when Mom realized what I had just said.

"*Thank You, Father, for answering my prayers! For our miracle!*" I prayed.

I looked at my two beautiful baby girls in the back seat. They were both sound asleep. Momma and I rejoiced all the way home.

God answers prayers, even when there doesn't seem to be a way. He is waiting for us to use our Faith when we pray. I looked at my burgundy Bible on the dashboard. I took it everywhere. I even write in it, when God answers a prayer. I learned that from my Momma.

I have every reason to believe that God put coins in the fish's mouth so that when he told the man to go and catch a fish, *that fish* was the one he caught.

GOD REMEMBERS

The month passed quickly. The kids were growing. Gary had his new job. He was doing well. It would be nice for him to work all winter for a change. Teri was five months old. I was planning a birthday party for Toni's second birthday coming up. Steve had just started school again. We saw Tracy once in awhile.

Early one August morning, I got up, poured myself a cup of coffee, and went out and sat in the porch swing. The children were still in bed. Not much going on today. I saw leaves on the big tree on the boulevard had turned the brightest yellow. The hummingbirds were buzzing around the feeder. I just sat there meditating, looking at the hanging pots full of flowers. I watched as the cardinals, blue jays, and other birds flew around in the trees. A fox squirrel came down the tree and found some acorns on the ground, he stuffed his cheeks, and scurried back up the tree.

"Thank you, Lord for what You have blessed us with." I prayed out loud.

So many things have been happening in our lives. I had recovered from having the baby. I got my strength back.

Our church was growing by leaps and bounds. In fact, they had to install wall cribs in the nursery because we had so many babies born in our congregation in the past two years. We hired a pastor a while back. He and his wife were very sweet people.

I reached down and petted the dog laying at my feet. Yes, life was good at the Stearns' home. I got up to refill my coffee cup. As I opened the front door, I hear Toni in her bed.

"Mommy! Tum dit me!"

"Good morning precious." I hugged her and then lift her out of the crib. She snuggled her head on my neck, as I held her. I sat on the sofa, gently playing with the curl on her forehead. I patted her back for a few minutes as we sat there.

After a few more minutes, I laid her on the couch and changed her diaper.

"Do you want to go to Grandma's house today?" I asked her.

"Yes, Mutho!" she said.

Mutho was the word for Mother, that Toni called me. She could not pronounce the letter r for some reason. The doctor just said she should grow out of it eventually. I learned there were others in Gary's family that couldn't say the letter r, also, when they were young.

"As soon as Bay Doll wakes up, we can get ready and go!" Toni got down off of the sofa and got her Lolly dolly, from her bed. She pretended to warm the bottle and then fed her baby.

Soon, Teri woke up and I bathed her and changed, both, her and Toni's clothes. We loaded up the diaper bag, and set off to Grandma's house.

I drove to Hurst, to visit Momma and Daddy. Daddy worked for himself, for the past years. He had opened a garage that he called *Smilin' Les' Alignment Shop*. He specialized in brakes, tires, and front-end alignments. He was a wonderful mechanic. He could rebuild a transmission or a motor. People even drove from Chicago, to have him work on their cars. He loved being at home with Momma all day too.

As we pulled up into the driveway, Momma was standing at the door. She came out and carried the baby into the house. I grabbed Toni and the diaper bag.

We got inside and got settled. Momma got her hugs from Toni and held the baby, as I poured us a cup of coffee. We sat in the living room and chatted about the weather, and other things. Mom always let me know what my sisters were all up to. She also showed me new pictures of my nephews and told me how they were doing in North Carolina. We talked for awhile and then Dad came in to see us. Toni ran to Grandpa with open arms.

"*Gwampa! I love you!*" She squealed as she jumped up on his lap. She hugged his neck. Daddy loved the kids. Momma got up to get him a cup of coffee. We chatted about things. Dad asked me what my plans were.

"I know you aren't one to be off work for very long." he said to me.

"Daddy, *I'm like a cat in a cage! I'm not sure what to do right now! Not many hiring until Christmas! I don't want to do sales right now! I'm not interested in working at the mall again! I'm really not sure what I would even want to do at this point! I have to make it worthwhile to even go back to the workplace! Especially since we have 4 kids now!*"

Momma soon came back into the living room with coffee cake and more coffee. We continued our conversation about my future.

Momma said, "You liked it at Walmart. Maybe you can work there again, but in another town."

"I don't think another town was what they meant when they said no one can be related and work in the company."

Mom finished her coffee cake, "I know! Why don't you go to school and be what you've always wanted to be?" I looked down and stirred my spoon in my coffee cup.

I looked at Dad . . . I looked over at Momma . . . I saw my two babies on the couch.

"I know God has been with me all of these years. He has shown me miracles and wonders. He has lead me down paths I didn't want to go . . . But to go to school and be what I always wanted to be? We don't have money. Gary will be off work soon. School? That sounds really good! But . . . It's been such a long time . . . I'm sorry, but . . . but, I really don't even remember what I even said I always wanted to be!"

Mom laughed as she replied, *"You may not know, but God remembers!"*

I drove home that day asking God to help make all my hopes and dreams come true . . .

NOT REALLY ~~ THE END

ACKNOWLEDGEMENTS

How can I not thank God in Heaven, first, for walking with us through all of the trials and tribulations, as well as the triumphs?

Thank you to my wonderful husband, Gary, who encourages me and stands beside me, as my rock and shield, through thick and thin. Thanks for continually reminding, me for the past thirty years, to write my book.

Thank you to all of my children, Toni, Teri, Tracy, and Steven, for putting up with your *crazy Momma* as I talked about writing a book for 30 years.

Thank you to all of the prayer warriors, over the years who have prayed for us when we were in the midst of the battles.

Thank you to all of the doctors and nurses, both locally (Dr. Janet Robinson) and the St Louis Children's Hospital Cystic Fibrosis medical team, who helped our daughter, Teri Lynn, with her medical issues. She is now married and is the mother of two young children.

A special thank you to Mary Cripps, for sharing your C. F. experience with Cole.

Thank you to Chandler Bolt, Sean Sumner, and all of the SPS Family, for the tips and videos that you share weekly, to help each of us, while we write and publish our books.

Special thank you to JS Shipman, for helping edit, to Jen Henderson, for formatting, and Fiverr, for creating my fantastic cover.

Thank you to my parents, Doris and Lester Darmstatter, in Heaven, for raising me in a Christian home, and teaching me to believe in myself, even when all odds were against me.

SELF-PUBLISHING
SCHOOL

NOW IT'S YOUR TURN

Discover the EXACT 3-step blueprint you need
to become a bestselling author in 3 months.

Self-Publishing School helped me, and now I want
them to help you with this FREE WEBINAR!

Even if you're busy, bad at writing, or don't know where to start,
you CAN write a bestseller and build your best life.

With tools and experience across a variety niches
and professions, Self-Publishing School is the only resource
you need to take your book to the finish line!

DON'T WAIT

Watch this FREE WEBINAR now, and
Say "YES" to becoming a bestseller:

https://xe172.isrefer.com/go/sps4fta-vts/bookbrosinc5136